On the Rim
of the Curve

A play about the Beothuks of Newfoundland.

CAST

AUTHOR

RINGMASTER

COURTIER
1st FURRIER
2nd FURRIER
INDIAN WOMAN
1st LADY
2nd LADY
INDIAN MAN
NONOSABASUT
BUSINESSMAN
PEYTON
LIEUT. BUCHANS
DEMASDUIT
ESAU
DANIEL
SIR HUMPHREY GILBERT
1st DANCER
2nd DANCER
SHANADITHIT

Europeans. Indians. As many or as few as the director wishes.
MUSICIANS: Up to three but not less than two. A musical score
is available from the author, who, however, would not limit production
by insisting upon its use... the score is open to a variety of
interpretations.

8

Michael
COOK

Three Plays

BREAKWATER
BOOKS, LTD. BOX 52, SITE C, PORTUGAL COVE, NEWFOUNDLAND A0A 3K0

Michael COOK

Three Plays:

On the Rim of the Curve

The Head, Guts and Soundbone Dance

Theresa's Creed

Copyright © by
Michael Cook

Published by
Breakwater Books Limited
P.O. Box 52, Site C,
Portugal Cove, Newfoundland
A0A 3K0

Printed in Canada by
Robinson - Blackmore Printing and Publishing Limited
18 O'Leary Avenue, St. John's, Newfoundland

Typeset by
Breakwater Books Limited

Cover design by
Peter BN Greenslade BDes AGDC

Rights to produce any of these plays in whole or in part, in any medium or by any group, amateur or professional, are retained by the author and interested persons are requested to apply to his agent, Madonna Decker, Box 327, Petley, Random Island, Newfoundland.

Canadian Cataloguing in Publication Data

Cook, Michael, 1933-
    Three plays

    Contents: The head, guts and soundbone dance.--
Theresa's creed.-- On the rim of the curve.
    ISBN 0-919948-30-8

I. Title: The head, guts and soundbone dance.
II. Title: Theresa's creed. III. Title: On the rim of
the curve.

PS8555.057A6 1977   C812'.'54   C77-000127-0

PR9199.3.C64A6 1977   78-2720

N.B.:   Whereas the full cast is desirable it may on occasion be necessary to double up where limited budgets and personnel make such a proposal inevitable, i.e. Furriers, Dancers, Esau and Daniel could be one and the same person.

SETTING.

A series of curved platforms are angled diagonally across the stage, the platforms ascending so that the last, left platform ends, literally, on the rim of a curve. The structures are supported on thick palings. Reminiscent of the type used by the Beothuck Indians to trap the caribou as they crossed the Exploits River in the Spring. Curved access ramps cut across the platforms right and left, making it possible for the actors to mount the platforms from back and centre stage. The centre ramp has no access, other than a walkway · connecting it to platforms right and left. It also has, built onto it, a slightly raised dais, with a curved railing, the Ringmaster's post. Beneath the centre piece, a sufficiently large gap in the support railings leaves sufficient space for the musicians, who remain on stage with their equipment throughout. Downstage right, between the triangle created by access ramp and platform, is a small wooden table and bench. In the equivalent space left, is a Mamateek, and assorted cooking implements.
Throughout the play the Europeans occupy the right platform, the Indians the left.

....

The lights rise. The company enter variously from left and right, making their way to their platforms. The author wanders in and out amongst them, checking the characters against a script, making sure they're all there. As they reach their positions they turn their backs upon the audience. Their silhouettes thrown against a backdrop of imprisoning bars. Throughout, a musician plays a high, wild, haunting melody on a flute, ceasing when all are in position. The author comes forward into a spotlight.

AUTHOR: Bear with me, friends, for friends I account all I don't know, and speaking across distances makes friendship even stronger. Voices, in cold Canada, are often all we have. God's life! I started to write a play, colours and contours filling the stage of the mind until they overflowed and fought like scavengers for their particular

9

images, before falling and folding into dreams made ghostly by the sun.

Look! I never knew my grandfather but it would be easy to write about him. There's something of him in my father and, ultimately, me, and we did, at least, share a common mythology of sorts. But how d'you write of a vanished people? Out of a bone? A book? A lock of hair? A litany of lies? Or simply honest confusion. Sooner write of Atlantis.

It seemed that even those who made contact with them, the Beothucks, the Red Men and Women, once the tribe had died, had slipped back into woods and leaf mould — why, then they seemed bemused, struggled for expression, wrestled with vanishing images as a man lifted from sleep reaches for the tail end of dreams and clutches at air, going on down to breakfast with nothing save a vague nausea troubling the stomach.

Don't misunderstand me. This isn't by way of being an apology. I'm just saying that there's no conclusion to this. None possible. Its a series of false starts, you might say, leading back to the central question that's never been asked.

I want you to help me piece the skeleton together, match bone to bone, let the dark flesh it out.

MUSICIAN: *One sustained, sharp, catatonic bar of music.*

AUTHOR: Is everything that happens to us determined in a dark past, making a mockery of will?

MUSICIAN: *Music mocking his question.*

AUTHOR: These ancient rocks, paleozoic, were not always naked to the blind heavens. Once, they slept warm beneath rich soil abundant with wild flowers until the earth tilted, cooled, and the ice raped the land.

MUSICIAN: *A shift in tone, chords rich and sonorous, speaking of distance.*

AUTHOR: Depositing the soil then, filtering down through the glittering water grain upon grain diffused, clouding the bitter Atlantic until after a time the Banks waited, agents of history.

MUSICIAN: *A repeat of the previous rich chords.*

AUTHOR: Looking back now with certain hindsight at the howling Basque, the Portuguese, the Profligate English, Irish, flying their Mediterranean Christ at the masthead, it all seems so logical. Ice. Soil. Fish. The gifts of destiny. The Beothuks failed to adapt. That's all.

MUSICIAN: *One thin reed pipe wail.*

AUTHOR: Question. Do you believe, with Plato, that the aggressor is more to be pitied than the victim of aggression? Are we deserving of such pity? I don't know.

MUSICIAN: *One thin reed pipe wail.*

AUTHOR: But perhaps they never existed at all. Were no more than an illuminated manuscript, painted by God on the rock in a weak moment. Then to be blurred by mist, colours running in the cold rain, images tumbling to the sea in the Spring of our coming, echoes of principalities and powers clinging to the forest, the lakes etched with the wake of dream.

MUSICIAN: *One thin reed pipe wail.*

AUTHOR: It is possible.... It is possible that they never existed at all.

MUSICIAN: *A prolonged drum roll.... The author exits, lights flare up on the European platform. The Ringmaster turns, raising his hands. The other Europeans turn, all clap, whistle, cheer, stamp their feet.*

RINGMASTER: Thank you, thank you, thank you. *(Drum roll and applause die.)* I am your Ringmaster for the evening, and, in our program we have for you voices of the past and present and , yes, even the future. Wild Sir Humphrey himself will claim the land. There will be furriers and fisherman, lusty brave lads of the old days, and our popular hero, old John Peyton himself who'd track an Indian for a month if they so much as stole a sail needle. *(The Europeans cheer, applaud. The Ringmaster waves for silence.)* Thank you again. There'll also be songs and dances and, yes, even a few prizes. So stay with it folks for we also have an Indian or two present and if you're good, you can all help pull the trigger... *(Europeans applaud.)* We'll trek up to Heaven and down to Hell, boys, but first, a word from our sponsor... the Beothuk Indians....

MUSICIAN: *A flute call... reminiscent of a bird. Lights go up slowly on the Indian platform. They remain backs turned, silent. The flute dies away... a thirty second silence....*

RINGMASTER: Thank you, my Red friends. And now, the Prologue.

MUSICIAN: *An Elizabethan air. A Courtier detaches himself and comes down the access ramp, sits at the table,and begins to write. Two Furriers leave the platform by the upstage ramp and come on round to peer over the Courtiers shoulder.*

COURTIER: *(Writing)* The people of the country of the New Found Land are very barbarous and uncivilised. They clothe themselves in the skins of beasts of which there are great plenty. They live in caverns of rocks and in houses shaped like birds' nests. They have no laws, believe much in auguries, and are very jealous of their wives.

1st FURRIER: How d'ye know?

COURTIER: What?

2nd FURRIER: He said, how d'ye know. Must've been after a piece of red, I'd say. *(Both laugh)*

COURTIER: I have it on extremely trustworthy report. *(Aside)* The insolence of the lower orders in this confounded place knows no bounds.

1st FURRIER: Oh. Jest reports, is it. Well, me friend here can add to yer book. Ned, Ned, b'y, when did ye last have an Indian woman.

2nd FURRIER: Oh now, let me see... why, that wor last evening, as I recall.

COURTIER: *(Excited)* Oh, really. Was she willing? Compliant? Enthusiastic?

2nd FURRIER: I dunno, b'y. She wor dead by the time I got to her. Still warm though, that's what counts.

Both laugh, and exit, laughing, back up to the platform. On the Indian platform, Beothuk woman turns....

INDIAN WOMAN: I sing a song of the salmon flicking the dark sea aside with his tail. He comes from beyond the place where the birds are. How far have you come to me, leaping into the sun to make rainbows? What God sent you to fatten the child in my belly?

MUSICIAN: *A simulated bird call.*

Two ladies detach themselves from European platform and come down stage, promenading centre.

COURTIER: *(Writing)* In this year were brought unto the King Henry, called old Nipcheese by some out of his hearing, three men taken in Newfoundland. They were clothed with beast skins and ate raw flesh and spoke in a language that no man could understand them, in their demeanour like to brute beasts whom the King kept for a time. Some two years past after, I saw two apparelled after the manner of English men in Westminster Palace, but as for speech, I heard none of them utter one word.

MUSICIAN: *Elizabethan air held under, softly, the following...*

1st LADY: I heard that Lady Mary has been seen several times of an evening with one of the Red Men. She claims... to be educating him in the courtly skills.

2nd LADY: She always did have a lust for the rude and the ignorant.

1st LADY: True. But setting one's cap low can often bring pleasure with some measure of safety.

2nd LADY: That's possible. But I think I'd rather risk my head than the pox, or some disgusting Indian disease. What satisfaction does she get from him. Have you heard?

1st LADY: Who should say. He cannot speak. And she does not choose to. But it can hardly be less than the silly Genovese got for bringing them back in the first place. *(Both laugh.) The music fades into one faint bird cry. On the Indian platform a man turns....*

INDIAN MAN: I sing a song of her who lay long with me in the liquid days. We cast one shadow sleeping. When she sang, the caribou lifted their heads in the high places, and were still. Moon. Throw my shadow to her across the big water.

MUSICIAN: *One faint simulated bird cry.*

COURTIER: *(Writing)* They are men of an indifferent stature, but wild and unruly. They wear their hair tied on top like a wreath of bay.

1st WOMAN: No, no, no. You've got it all wrong. They are full eyed, of a black colour. The colour of their hair is diverse, some black, some brown, some yellow. And their faces are flat and broad.

COURTIER: *(Writing)* Terra Nova of the codfish is a cold place. The inhabitants are idolators, some worshipping the sun, others the moon, and many other kinds of idols. It is a fair race but savage.

2nd WOMAN: The Venetian says that the new lands are the territory of the Grand Cham....

Both laugh.... Promenade. A soft, insistent drum roll begins. The Courtier closes his book, crosses to and joins the ladies. Their dialogue, from this point on begins to match the pacing and delivery of the drum roll, becoming increasingly staccato.

COURTIER: They do say the Indians are idolators.

1st WOMAN: They pray to the sun, and the moon, and diverse idols.

COURTIER: It is certain that by establishing a plantation in Trinity, the poor misbelieving inhabitants of that wretched country may be reduced from barbarism to a knowledge of God.

2nd WOMAN: The country is sterile and uncultivated, producing nothing, from which circumstance it happens that it is crowded with white bears and stags of an unusual height and size.

COURTIER: The people are very barbarous and uncivilised.

1st WOMAN: The inhabitants are idolators.

COURTIER: A fair race but savage.

2nd WOMAN: A cold place.

COURTIER: Some actually worship the sun. Others the moon.

1st WOMAN: We must bring them to a knowledge of God.... *(The three of them repeat the line...)* We must bring them to a knowledge of God.

Drum roll suddenly ceases. A second Indian Woman turns on her platform....

INDIAN WOMAN: In the beginning, child, was the bow, and the Bow was God, and the bow was with God. You must learn to sing of the Bow and the arrows falling like stars. We are the children of the Bow, the children of the stars. Our coming was mirrored in water, only the water mirrors our passing.

MUSICIAN: *Drum roll begins softly again, beneath the following.*

COURTIER: *(Looking up at Indian ramp)* Behold. The untutored Indian whose untutored mind sees God in the clouds, or hears him in the winds.

1st WOMAN: They have some knowledge of a Supreme Being.

2nd WOMAN: They hear God in the wind.

COURTIER: They actually believe that men and women were originally created by a number of arrows being stuck fast in the ground.

1st WOMAN: Cold.

COURTIER: Barbarous.

2nd WOMAN: Uncivilised.

COURTIER: Idolators.

1st WOMAN: Beast skins.

COURTIER: Never speak.

2nd WOMAN: Jealous.

COURTIER: Naked.

1st WOMAN: Full breasted.

COURTIER: Goodly stature.

2nd WOMAN: Some golden haired.

COURTIER: They smell.

1st WOMAN: Red Indians.

COURTIER: Must bring them to knowledge.

2nd WOMAN: A knowledge of God.

COURTIER: But they smell.

1st WOMAN: Painted with filth.

COURTIER: Red... Indians.

2nd WOMAN: They steal.

COURTIER: Fornicate privately.

1st WOMAN: Heathens.

COURTIER: Head hunters.

2nd WOMAN: They steal....

COURTIER: We must bring them to knowledge.... *(All three....)* To a knowledge of God.

The drum roll reaches its peak. Ends with the abruptness of a pistol shot. An Indian Woman detaches herself from the platform and runs down centre stage, dodging through the Courtly Trio. At the same time, the two Furriers roar down the European ramp, carrying muskets, in pursuit.

1st FURRIER: There she goes.

2nd FURRIER: Head her off.

They chase her about centre stage. Once again she tries to dodge through the Courtly Trio, but one of the women trips her as she seeks to burst through. The Trio breaks to make way for the Furriers. The Indian Woman lies sprawling.

1st FURRIER: *(Threatening her with musket.)* Kneel, ye bitch. Kneel. *(The woman turns and kneels.)*

2nd FURRIER: Thats it. Now lets see yer tits. *(The woman, with great dignity, slowly bares her breasts.)*

1st FURRIER: Mother of God. She's pregnant.

2nd FURRIER: This'll stop her breeding. *(He fires at her, point blank. She topples slowly. There is a slight movement. An infant discovered under the Indian platform.)*

1st FURRIER: Look. Another one. A baby.

2nd FURRIER: Where.

1st FURRIER: Crawling through the brush.

2nd FURRIER: Fire, man, fire. Don't let the little bastard get away. *(Courtier and the two Ladies, in unison...)* Fire, man. Fire. *(The 1st Furrier takes aim and fires.)*

1st FURRIER: That's done fer it. *(They turn back to the dead woman. 2nd Furrier kneels and inspects her.)*

2nd FURRIER: Jesus. She had some set on her. Look. The milk's running out.

1st FURRIER: I s'pose we could've waited a bit. Made some use of her.

2nd FURRIER: Fer God's sake, b'y, they stink worse'n old ewe. Come on. They's more up ahead.

1st FURRIER: Won't we throw 'em into the lake.

2nd FURRIER: No, b'y. They's half rotten already. Just leave 'er wi' her brat under the bushes. *(They drag the woman beneath the*

ramp, come back, shoulder their muskets and begin to march about
centre stage singing...) Heigh Ho, Heigh Ho, its off to work we go, As
the red men run we fire our guns Heigh Ho, Heigh Ho, Heigh Ho,
Heigh Ho.
They are joined by the Courtier and the two Ladies, singing, they
march   back   up   the   centre   ramp   to   their   platform.
MUSICIAN: *The wild, high lament, as at opening of play. The*
lights dim on all areas. Single spotlight illuminates Nonasabust who
turns.

NONASABASUT: I, Nonasabasut, laboured to free
myself of the old mortality,
the   obsession   with   wind   and   stars,
her   body,   salmon   silver   in   moonlight.
I atoned for blood,
the blood of my enemies,
the blood of caribou and bear,
the cold blood of fishes.

I rendered up
the gift of mysteries,
my inheritance,
the   knowledge   of   water   and   birds,
the conversation of trees.

And   now,   on   the   rim   of   the   curve
when all should be one,
wife, child, self, the People
spirit moulded to spirit,
daring the final journey,
the unspeakable regions,
I am troubled once more
with lost voices, the ancient
thunder of dying.
I am tired, Father,
of sifting that truth for meaning.

MUSICIAN: *A jangling, faint metallic sound, as of the clashing of*
stars or spears.
NONASABASUT: I am tired of drowning in old deaths.
MUSICIAN: *As before.*
NONASABASUT: The   milk   of   her   breasts   frozen,
nipples   stiff   with   frost   and   fear,
the   bloody   hand   of   the   cruel   one

squeezing, squeezing that roundness
as if her milk could warm him.

MUSICIAN: *As before.... A little more prolonged, echoing.*

NONASABASUT: I am tired
of my external surprise
leaning into her picture,
one hand on his throat,
the other reaching for her,
feeling the stab in the back,
the shot in the back,
the hole in the chest,
watching the water of my body
slip and freeze on my hands,
the tented fabric of dreams folding.

MUSICIAN: *As before.*

NONASABASUT: Do not keep us alive
in the minds of men,
or let their dreams
arrest our journey.
It was a good destiny
I have learned,
we walking in sleep
not to wake in the New World,
and those grim men,
grey arrows sped on your breath
became our saviours
and the inheritors of our suffering.
For we were what we were
and nothing changed us
from our coming to our going.

MUSICIAN: *As before.*

NONASABASUT: Let us pass on.

MUSICIAN: *Drumming, as of a persistent wind... increasing in intensity.... The light fades on Nonasabasut, goes up on the Ringmaster and the European platform.*

RINGMASTER: *(Shouting)* Hey.... Hey, what's going on. Stop that wind. Fasten the tent pegs. Did you hear something.... I heard something and whatever it was I didn't like it. Gave me quite a turn for a moment.

MUSICIAN: *Drumming slows and softens.... from the shadows on the Indian platform.*

NONASABASUT: Let us pass on.

All the Indians on their platform, softly, in unison....

INDIANS: Let us pass on.... *(The drumming fades, stops....)*

RINGMASTER: *(Wiping his brow.)* I must have been imagining things. Happens, you know, in the entertainment business. Its a tough business. We have to keep on top of it, though. Now, let us pass on... and to set the tone for the first act, lets give a big hand to the furriers quartet....

All the occupants of the European platform cheer, whistle, stamp. The quartet, smirking, make their way to the edge of the platform and face out. Their song is sung to the tune of 'Drake is Going West, Lads.' They start as in a barbers' quartet, then ramble into the song....

QUARTET: We're going down the Exploits....

We're going down the Exploits....
We're going down the Exploits River....

We're going down the Exploits,
You'd like to go, would you,
Then go you shall
to share the fight,
And the Glory too,
Before our guns the foe will fly,
women, children too,
For we're away at break of day
to hunt, to hunt the heathens down....

All on the platform join in the chorus....

EUROPEAN COMPANY: Then here's to the river wide,
And here's to the fray,
And here's to Peyton's merry, merry men
Who won't come back to the Bay again
Till they've skinned the enemy's hide.

The quartet start into the second verse going into their barbers routine, but after the third line are interrupted. A businessman detaches himself from the European group and proceeds down the ramp. Goes up stage centre and calls up to the ringmaster.

BUSINESSMAN: What kind of a show did you say this was. Did you say it was a Red Indian show.

RINGMASTER: Did I say Red. Red.

BUSINESSMAN: That's right, Sir. Red.

RINGMASTER: Ladies and gentlemen. This neatly dressed, middle aged, slightly greying, military moustached, rather paunchy but otherwise fairly trim executive type asks me whether I said Red. *All laugh*.

RINGMASTER: What, sir, did you think I said?

BUSINESSMAN: I thought you said, dead.

RINGMASTER: *(Triumphant)* And dead, Sir, is what I did say, if not in fact by inference and you, Sir, are the winner of this skull found by a bulldozer operator in Northern Newfoundland and used as a pipe holder until saved for posterity by a keen eyed Lady American tourist....

Ringmaster throws down a skull. It is clearly dyed with red ochre. The man catches it, and holds on to it gingerly while the remainder applaud.

BUSINESSMAN: Its very nice. Very nice, indeed. But I wouldn't know where to hang it. My wife has a mortal fear of all things to do with death, Sir, and has been known to burst into tears when I've had occasion to kill the house flies that plague us in July month.

RINGMASTER: He wouldn't know where to hang it. And his wife is blessed with a love of all things, all creatures great and small. *(A communal sigh)*.

BUSINESSMAN: I didn't know she was blessed with a love of all things. That's not what I said at all. There are many things she possibly detests, including me. She doesn't like to see them killed, that's all. Providing the murderous act takes place out of sight, she's quite happy.

RINGMASTER: See no evil, hear no evil...?

BUSINESSMAN: Exactly.

RINGMASTER: She is, Sir, obviously, a model of circumspection. Do you have a den?

BUSINESSMAN: Of course I have. Its a very nice den as a matter of fact. Lined with leather bound copies of the Readers Digest... Canadian edition of course....

RINGMASTER: Of course....

ALL: Of course....

BUSINESSMAN: A nylon bear skin hangs over the wall, and an antique replica of a sealing musket, circa 1819 is nailed, at a jaunty angle above a well stocked bar.

ALL EUROPEANS: *Applaud*.

BUSINESSMAN: *(Gratified)* Thank you... thank you very much.

RINGMASTER: You, Sir, have solved your own problem, for what better place than a unique Canadian den for this superbly mounted faithful photographic reproduction of this Red Indian, Nonasabasut by name, killed while unlawfully attempting to rescue his wife from the King's agents. *(Calling)* Lads....

Two members of the European group move rapidly to Ringmaster at centre ramp, where they pick up and unroll a hugh photographic replica of Nonasabasut lying dead on the ice... his wife, held by furriers, looks on. The businessman goes up the ramp, crosses to Ringmaster, shakes his hand. The photograph is rolled up and presented to him. All cheer, whistle, applaud.

BUSINESSMAN: You're absolutely right, of course. The den is the very place for it. Its very nice. Very nice, indeed. And Mary would never intrude down there. Some things are still **sacred**, thank God.

MUSICIAN: *Sound as of a hunting call... repeated. An Indian woman comes down slowly from Indian platform, stands centre, turns slowly in a circle. All Europeans with the exception of the Ringmaster and the Businessman move down upstage and downstage ramps and circle her.*

INDIAN WOMAN: Newin.... Newin.... Newin....

BUSINESSMAN: Good God. What is that woman doing down there in the ring.

RINGMASTER: *(Consulting a watch)* She's right on time. Excellent. But that, Sir, is not a woman. That... is a Red Indian. She and the men encircling her are about to re-enact an Indian hunt as it took place some hundred and fifty years ago....

MUSICIAN: *The hunting call. Repeated.*

In slow motion the woman moves in and out of the circle, amongst the stakes supporting the platforms. Pursued in slow motion by the Europeans. A dance of death.

RINGMASTER: She's trying to dodge amongst the firs, the spruce, the birch. She's praying for a storm, a thunderclap, for the earth to open beneath her pursuer's feet. She is wishing that the men hadn't left her to go hunting the caribou, that her mother wasn't so sick and feeble that she was unable to go with them. She is remembering bright mornings with her man in a canoe on the lake, the warm sun drawing a mist from the water soft as thistledown, cool as a first kiss. She sees again the partridge trapped in its cage of ice after the first glitter storm of the fall. She hears again her laughter as she flees her lover into the woods, knowing the spot by the moss rock where he will catch her and they will cleave to the ground. She is remembering the child at her breast, the one who died coughing, and the eyes of her man grown fearful and distant, as one who sees a world's end in one infant's loss. *The Indian woman emerges, backing centre. The Europeans stalk her in a half circle. The lights dim until there are nothing but shadows and silhouettes stilled, posed in a tableau. Spot remains on Ringmaster....*

BUSINESSMAN: She's stopped.

RINGMASTER: Ah, yes. This is the moment we've all been waiting for.

INDIAN WOMAN: Newin.... Newin....

BUSINESSMAN: I do believe she's bearing her breasts. *(Peering down)* She is. Disgusting. I didn't come here for a strip show. What would my wife say. Breasts are dirty....

RINGMASTER: And Indian breasts are disgustingly dirty. I agree, I agree, but don't distress yourself unduly. She won't get away with it. She's bearing her breasts for mercy, you see. She's turning on her knees, showing them to the crowd, arms outstretched. There. The hunters are poised about her, a living tableau. What control. What discipline. They're hardly breathing.

MUSICIAN: *Faint... a repeat of the hunter call....*

RINGMASTER: This is the moment of truth. For them. For her. What is your decision.

BUSINESSMAN: My decision?

RINGMASTER: Its your show.

INDIAN WOMAN: Newin... Newin....

We are aware of all faces half turned, expectant, up towards the Businessman. With a sudden gesture he raises both his hands, then turns them thumbs down.

RINGMASTER: Good man. *(Shouting down)* Appeal rejected. *A roar from the crowd below, an animal growl, then a rush of movement surrounding, trampling, beating, washing over the Indian Woman. She screams once.... A high bubbling scream.... The movement is stilled. There is silence.*

RINGMASTER: Well, that takes care of that. Another triumph for decency. What did you think of that, Sir. What would your good wife think of that?

BUSINESSMAN: I don't know, really. It was pretty well done, I must say. She'll enjoy me telling her about it. She'll probably get quite excited. Is there more...?

RINGMASTER: *More, he says. Is there more...*

MUSICIAN: *Beginning drum roll... it builds through the following.*

BUSINESSMAN: What's that...?

RINGMASTER: Better get back to your place now. Ye don't want to get washed away by the tide, or history or both. And take your

photograph... don't forget your photograph. *(Turning)* To your places
e v e r y o n e ...   to   y o u r   p l a c e s .   We   m u s t   p a s s   o n ....
The drums build to a climax. The Europeans go back to their platform
with the exception of Peyton, who goes to the table. Lights fade on
Ringmaster, come up on area to the right. Peyton is writing to the
Governor — finished, stands up, reads aloud.

PEYTON: Dear Governor,

I have the Honour to report that in our attempts to make contact
and communication with the Native Indian tribe of this island, on
your express orders and with the promise of the bounty in mind so
generously offered by yourself on behalf of His Gracious Majesty....
Mm. I like that. Has a proper touch about it. Bit o' cap pulling in the
introduction followed by a nice piece of hand washing.... Good. *(Reads*
again) Myself and my men, being fitted out at considerable expense,
and losing much time at the fishing and fur trade into the bargain,
went down the Exploits on our mission of peace and Christain charity
in search of the said tribe... the Beothuk Indians. The weather was
none too good fer the time of the year, heavy rain and strong South
Westerly's had swollen the river and made the going difficult, and we
about to turn back, the men mindful of the lawful profit they were
losing when we came across a Red Woman, I'm afraid to say, Your
Honour, clad in a shameless garb that barely covered her nameless
parts.... *(Breaks off)* Lets him know that we're decent men up here
though we lack regular church, and there's little law save our own,
Thank God. Nameless parts... *(Chuckles. Returns to the letter)*
... and in addition, a garment exposing those organs that were
designed by God's will for the sole and express purpose of succouring
the innocent....

(Breaks off, chuckling) That's delicate. That's a turn of phrase worthy
of a magistrate. *(Reads again)* This woman, alas, did solicit not only
my men, but myself, and, as it happened, came upon us when we,
having abandoned all hope of our mission, had paused to trap a few of
God's creatures for profit and His greater glory.... Needless to say, I
exhorted her, in sign language, not to inflame my poor fellows baser
passions... they being but simple folk, more open to sin than the more
worthy and literate amongst us whom a higher purpose has called to
accomplish greater things on behalf of His Most Christian Majesty....
And so it did fall out that she did wrestle one of my poor brown lads to
the ground, I do believe for an immoral purpose which decency forbids
me to mention, and in his falling, his gun did accidently discharge and
she was inadvertently killed, a large portion of her anatomy, to wit,

that which God had ordained to succour the innocent being blown a distance of some thirty feet, coming to rest in a clump of balsam fir. It was with difficulty that I restored my men to order, so distraught were they, weeping so they were not fit for men's work, but I prevailed upon them to give the woman a decent burial, and I myself read a few short words over her, though God knows, they will do the creature little comfort, as Baptism in the Holy Church was as far from her as it had ever been. My own feelings were that this affair was instigated by the woman's own immodesty. Oh, for a Man of God to be able to live amongst these people, as did the good Jesuits amongst the Iroquis, and at the beginning at least, instill in them some sense of morality and decency. I have the honour to be Sir, your obedient servant....
Lieutenant Buchans hurries down from the European ramp.

BUCHANS: Mr. Peyton.... Mr. Peyton....

PEYTON: Come in, Sir. Come in. The ship is in no trouble, I hope.

BUCHANS: No, sir. 'Tis not that at all. The ship is well founded but I fear these winds will keep us off shore for a good day or two.

PEYTON: Well, there's nothing to worry about then, Lieutenant. 'Tis true, my men are idle at the stores, but they do their best to be idle when I'm there... 'tis hard to find men who'll stick at anything for more than a day or two these times. Things aren't what they used to be, Sir. No. Men don't seem to know their place as they used to. Will ye join me in a glass?

BUCHANS: No, thank 'ee, Sir. My own crew are not too familiar with these waters, and I need to be on deck. No. I'm worried about the Indian Woman, Demasduit.

PEYTON: Oh, aye. The old one.

BUCHANS: She is ill. She cries out constantly, though whether in pain or some savage song or lament I cannot tell. If she were to die before we put ashore at Exploits, then our mission can be counted a failure.

PEYTON: Failure. Come, Sir. Dead or alive, her people will come for her.

BUCHANS: You don't seem to understand, Mr. Peyton. The Governor is critically anxious that we make amends for the damage done in the past. That we get her home alive, as a sign of good faith, that we might win the Indians' trust.

PEYTON: *(Laughing)* Well, Sir, I allows its probably a little late for that, but there's no harm in trying, I suppose. But that old one... ach, she's well past her prime. I told them it were hardly worth bringing her in in the first place, but who am I to disobey orders.

BUCHANS: You're a model citizen, Mr. Peyton.

PEYTON: Why... thank 'e, Sir.

BUCHANS: Let's stop beating about the bush, shall we? I'll be blunt. Its been reported by some of my crew that your men are already referring to the chest of presents for the tribe as their own. Its also been rumoured that they would murder the woman if they could, and throw her overboard. Now what have you to say.

PEYTON: Now that's a pernicious lie, Sir, that's what I say. Why, men are rough, yes. Murderous, never. Why, sir, I've only to speak from the side of me mouth to make 'em jump, and as for killing... 'tis unthinkable. 'Tis as much as I can do to get them to kill the animals what's their livelihood, they're that soft hearted. You may believe all the wild tales ye want, Lieutenant, but 'tis slanderous of ye to bring 'em to me.

BUCHANS: Ye may call it what the Hell you like, Peyton. I tell you, I know what's been going on, and if I can ever gather sufficient proof against you, or your men....

PEYTON: Now that's the trouble, sir, with your kind, for ye come in here with yer fancy notions of right and wrong and ye knows nothing about the way things are. The way they always was. Everyone talks too much most of the time about her, and them that does the talking doesn't know their arse from a hole in the ground if ye'll forgive my bluntness. They're a simple, superstitious, jealous lot about this coast, Sir, and if they think they can get the jump on a man and lay claim to his holdings by getting him out of the way, why then, they'll say or do anything....

BUCHANS: On their deathbed?

PEYTON: Men have been known to try and cheat their way to Heaven.

BUCHANS: And others have been known to lie their way to Hell.

PEYTON: *(Laughing)* Well, neither of us is too close to either place yet, I'd say. Now, I knows you're in command and that ye carry the law up this coast. But let me give you a word of advice, Mr. Buchans. There's men here have lost their friends; there's men here have stumbled over the head of a mate a year after he's disappeared, shrunken and shrivelled like a walnut. There's men here carrying scars from arrows and spears and there's men remembers ye, Lieutenant Buchans, and how ye left two poor souls alone with them savages... oh, out of ignorance of their ways, I'm sure, but ye must admit, when ye come back for 'em, they weren't a pretty sight.

BUCHANS: Mr. Peyton, I don't need a lecture from you on the

nature of either your men or the Red Indians. Nor do I need to be fed excuses for the vicious warfare you've been carrying on against them... a warfare I suspect that led directly to the deaths of my own men.*(Peyton moves to interrupt)* No, Sir. You must hear me out. You might carry the Governor's seal now, but I'm not the only one who is aware that you are one of the principals that made protection necessary.

PEYTON: Suspect away. I was about to tell ye, before ye got carried away, though God knows why I should bother to warn ye. If ye banish or hang a man on this coast for killing an Indian, Mr. Buchans, there's no telling what might happen to ye. *(Buchans turns to leave in disgust).*

PEYTON: And I hope the wind keeps off shore for a week until the stink of the woman sweeps into the timbers of yer boat so that ye never gets it out. Then see who'll heave her overboard, eh, Lieutenant. *From the Indian platform, in semi darkness... a piercing wail. It is Demasduit.*

PEYTON: There she goes. They all die in captivity, Lieutenant. I told the Governor the same thing. They'd rather be killed than taken or kept like dogs on a chain.

BUCHANS: I'm warning you, Peyton. You stick to order. And make sure your men do the same. And remember, on this ship, they're my orders.

PEYTON: On this ship... yes, Sir!

Demasduit wails again. Buchans hurries up the ramp, pausing as the wail comes again...

PEYTON: *(Shouting)* Get to her. That's the death wail. And if ye wants my men to carry the coffin to an Indian camp ye'll have to learn to be a trifle more civil, Mr. Buchans. Much more civil.... *Buchans takes his place on the ramp. Peyton, after a moment, laughs, exits, going back on to the platform via the rear ramp. Spotlight rises on Demasduit... downstage area dims. A half light rises on the Mamateek. An Indian Woman and man are discovered, sitting still, silent.*

DEMASDUIT: It is good to be tired,
It is good to be home.
To be buried between the cleft in
the rock, the womb of the rock
beneath stars,
to become tangled amongst
the roots of trees.

to succour the roots of trees,
to speed to life the moss,
the summer grasses,
the beetle scrambling for light.
I am sorry, my daughter,
I am past grief or grieving.
The warriors are waiting,
their backs bowed,
a living staircase.
The forest unrolls before me,
the rivers unwind,
the caribou flee
amongst stars.
Take up the ashes of your fire
and give the mamateeks
to the North wind,
gather the corners
of the world to your soul
 for the green days are done
and there is no place
left for us.

MUSICIAN: *One thin, high piping reed wail.*

INDIAN WOMAN: What do you hear, husband?

INDIAN MAN: Only a star falling.

INDIAN WOMAN: A star falling? It wakes the child. It sweats with fear. I have seen stars fall, but they make no sound.

DEMASDUIT: *Her death cry.*

INDIAN WOMAN: There it is again. Did you not hear it?

INDIAN MAN: It was a tree, splitting in the forest.

INDIAN WOMAN: A tree? Splitting in the forest? Look, the child is crying. And there is no frost. No ice on the water.

DEMASDUIT: *Her death cry.*

INDIAN MAN: Ah. I hear it now.

INDIAN WOMAN: It is the flesh failing.

INDIAN MAN: That is the right answer. Look. The child is asleep now. There is dirt in his mouth.

INDIAN WOMAN: There is a worm in his eye.

DEMASDUIT: *Her last, fading cry.*

MUSICIAN: *One thin, high piping reed wail.*

Lights fade on the Indian platform. On the mamateek. Spotlight up on the Ringmaster.

RINGMASTER: Welcome back, welcome back. For those of you interested, the woman, Demasduit, did die of course, and they dumped her and a big box of presents by the side of the river and they came and took her, her people, just like old Man Peyton said. Though they do say that most of the presents were gone by the time the Indians came to bury her according to their lights. Poor Lieutenant Buchans, he didn't do too well in these waters. Apart from leaving his marines to get their heads cut off, he seemed to feel more for the red skins than he did for his own countrymen. A hard driving man he was, and there were hard men set against him, too. He left under a bit of a cloud you might say. Unimportant man, really, he neither killed 'em or saved 'em, but he did give his name to a town, a mining town where for years the miners, the inheritors you might say, was treated like the Indians was treated. Funny, that. How the conquerors take on the role of the conquered. But enough lies. This is, after all, an entertainment, and its intermission. Time for a story.... Here in the big-top scantily dressed ladies dressed in Indian garb are moving about selling peanuts and ice cream and cookies and authentically crafted replicas of birch bark canoes made in Hong Kong.... *(As he is speaking the house lights go up to half, and ushers proceed according to his instructions).* We'll move into Act Two in a minute, but listen, as I was on my way to the show tonight I met these two fellers... what a story.... Well, there was these Red Indians see, and they was asleep in their tents, mamateeks or some such heathenish thing they called them, and this couple of fellers... I can hardly go on for laughing at the memory of it... these two... furriers they were, crept up on 'em in the night and set fire to their tent.... *(He laughs)* Well, if you could have seen it, eh? The Indians leaping out of their tent clutching their arses and the boys waiting outside to pick 'em off in the glare of the flames. Some sport, eh? Picked 'em off just like that, as they came dancing out of their tents clutching their rear ends. Funniest thing you ever did see, them fellers said....*(Laughs)* Now, has anyone else got a story for us while you are finishing yer ice cream. Has anyone a genuine, authentic Red Indian story.... *Two men detach themselves from the European platform and come down centre stage... they blink nervously out at the audience, back up at the Ringmaster....)*Why, yes, we have two volunteers, two gentlemen now at Centre stage, good solid looking citizens, the pair of them. Give them a big hand folks.... *(The company of Europeans whistle, stamp, applaud, cheer).*

RINGMASTER: And what's yer names, boys?

DANIEL: He's Esau.

27

ESAU: And he's Daniel.

RINGMASTER: And where are ye from, boys.

DANIEL: Tell him, Esau.

ESAU: I don't want to, Daniel.

RINGMASTER: Come on, come on, come on. We're all friends here. No secrets here. We've all paid to get in. We're entitled to know.

DANIEL: It don't matter to no one but us.

ESAU: We made a pact.

DANIEL: Its better that way.

ESAU: Its safer that way.

DANIEL: And it didn't happen to us.

ESAU: No. It didn't happen to us.

DANIEL: Just someone we knew.

ESAU: Someone who saw it happen to someone else.

DANIEL: But its not the kind of thing you want to carry alone.

ESAU: No. It needs to be shared.

DANIEL: Everybody lifting together.

ESAU: Everybody hauling together.

DANIEL: Singing.

ESAU: That way, ye can fergit it when yer awake.

DANIEL: But it helps to share it at night, too.

RINGMASTER: Well. What happened, man? What's the story? We're all waiting. Time's **running out**. This isn't one of your long nights by a winters fireside you know....

ESAU: Take out the lights, then.

RINGMASTER: Take out the lights! I can't do that. People might get frightened.

DANIEL: Take out the lights. Or no story.

RINGMASTER: **Alright**, alright. *(Shouting)* Technicians. Lights. Cut the lights.

The house lights go off. Light dims on Ringmaster. Esau and Daniel break left and right respectively.

RINGMASTER: Hey! Where are you two going.

DANIEL: To tell the story.

ESAU: You'll hear it.

DANIEL: Better this way.

ESAU: Safer this way.

Lights fade on Ringmaster. Single spots respectively on the faces of Esau and Daniel. Blackness between.

DANIEL: First off... it was night.

ESAU: We'd been trapping all day... the country....

DANEIL: Hard under foot. Tripping, sucking, clutchin', pulling...

ESAU: Tearing. Wrenching.

DANIEL: Come on to rain. Drops big as stones.

ESAU: Go through a man.

DANIEL: Put the fire out.

ESAU: One went for wood. Dry wood.

DANIEL: He never come back.

ESAU: We heard him call. Like an owl.

DANIEL: No, no. It were like a loon.

ESAU: Always liked to copy birds.

DANIEL: And when the sun come up, his empty space.

ESAU: We knew they'd got him.

DANIEL: The Indians had got him.

ESAU: Moved the woods at night.

DANIEL: Bent the rivers.

ESAU: Lured him on until he wor lost.

DANIEL: To walk into a clearing and find nothing but them, staring.

ESAU: We thought about him all year. Missed his bird cries.

DANIEL: The space by the side of us.

ESAU: His share, waiting.

DANIEL: Come spring, when the ice moved out, we moved in.

ESAU: Rowing steadily up the river.

DANIEL: The sun coming at ye from the tall trees.

A dim light goes up on the Indian platform.

ESAU: Seals playing.

DANIEL: Beavers starting to work.

ESAU: Trout thicker'n yer leg.

DANIEL: And a shouting....

ESAU: And a hollerin'....

DANIEL: And the trees parting like someone had slashed 'em wid a knife.

A movement on the ramp.... A man appears through a cluster of Indians... looks out, puts his hands to his mouth... makes a bird cry....

ESAU: And there he was.... Made a cry like a loon.

DANIEL: No, no, no. It wor like an owl.

ESAU: But we knew it wor him.

DANIEL: Beard a mile long.

ESAU: Dressed in rags and Indian clothes.

DANIEL: Leapt into the river and begun to swim.

The figure leaps off the Indian platform into the dark.

ESAU: We turned the boat toward him. Shouting.

DANIEL: We were some thrilled, I'll tell ye. It wor like a friend come back from the dead.

ESAU: And then, behind him, the trees parting and Indians....
On the platform, two or three Indians turn and face out.

DANIEL: Just standing there.

ESAU: We raised our muskets.

DANIEL: Didn't fire, though, fer fear they'd put an arrow through him.
Breaking through the group of Indians on the platform, a woman, carrying a baby.

ESAU: And then the woman come.

DANIEL: Aye, then the woman come.

ESAU: Carrying a baby.

DANIEL: I'd say three months old.

ESAU: I'd say two....

DANIEL: Give or take a week....

ESAU: 'Twas difficult to tell.

DANIEL: Lifted'n up fer all of us to see'n.
The woman lifts up the child.

ESAU: Lifted'n up for him to see'n as we hauled him dripping aboard.

DANIEL: Still didn't fire, though.

ESAU: She holding up the baby.

DANIEL: Him blubbering like a baby as we hauled him aboard.
"Fer the love of suffering Christ, get moving, get moving," he shouted.

DANIEL: And we started rowing.

ESAU: And the woman saw us rowing.

DANIEL: Took a knife from the hunter....
The woman takes a knife....

ESAU: The feller next to her... tall man. Blond, he seemed.

DANIEL: Red head, I thought....

ESAU: One or t'other... the sun wor blinding....

DANIEL: She raised the knife....
The woman does so.

ESAU: Cut the child in half....
She hacks the child in half.

DANIEL: I can hear it scream....

ESAU: I can hear her moan....

DANIEL: T'rew one half into the water....
The woman throws half the child into the dark.

ESAU: After him, see.

DANIEL: Took the other half back into the bush.

ESAU: Clutched to her, the other half....

The woman turns, the warriors close ranks, also turn their backs, the lights fade on the Indian platform.

DANIEL: Oh. We fired off a volley then.

ESAU: It were kind of half hearted....

DANIEL: The water come after us....

ESAU: The half a baby come after us.

DANIEL: Against the current....

ESAU: For the love of suffering Jesus!

DANIEL: He never did whistle after that. Made no more bird cries.

ESAU: Nor sing neither.

DANIEL: He left.

ESAU: No one knows where he come from.

DANIEL: Or where he's gone to.

ESAU: That's our story.

DANIEL: It needs to be shared.

ESAU: Help us.

Lights blackout. In the blackout, music, one sharp jangling bitter string.... It echoes on into silence... in the blackout Esau and Daniel regain the platform in the dark.

RINGMASTER: *(Shouting)* That's not a funny story.... You'll get no prizes for that story. Lights. Lights. Where the hell are those lights... who's messing about with them? We've got to get on.... *A dim light rises on the mamateek... the Indian woman is singing rocking, holding to her half the baby....*

INDIAN WOMAN: They didn't know what to do with him. My brothers. The white man was very frightened. The rain made him smell. The smell of fear steamed from him. The old one was for killing him. He argued and shouted, coughing until the blood ran from his mouth and we had to lay him down, hating his weakness, hating his age, defiant in dying. "Kill him as he has killed us," he whispered, the red froth bubbling at the corners of his fallen mouth like flood water over stones.

"You have no man," said my brother. And it was true. He was killed by the white men at the Bay of Seals. I remember lying in my husband's blood. It was warm to my back. And his killers tearing at me, one holding me down, holding my arms, while the others, four, five... its no matter. They soiled every part of my body.

"Take the white man," said my brother, "For no man of the tribe will fill your belly."

And I took him. I showed him the secret paths of the caribou, and pools where salmon slept all winter long. I bathed his wounds in the blood of berries and each night lay in a pool of my husband's blood. When the child moved within me I was fearful. Blood begets blood....
The lights fade on the mamateek....

MUSICIAN: *A drum roll... growing in intensity...*

RINGMASTER: *(In darkness)* Patience. Patience. Don't leave, anybody. Not yet. Somebody's monkeying around with the power cables. Some prankster. Some Indian no doubt, cutting, stealing, prowling....

The lights blaze on. The drum roll ceases.

RINGMASTER: *(Blinking)* Ah.... That's better. There we go, back to normal at last. Well, the intermission's ended, you can be sure of that. Its time for Act Two and here is the star you've all been waiting for, that well known historical hero, adventurer, man of letters, courtier, gallant, and wit, Wild Sir Humphrey Gilbert.... Give him a round, Ladies and Gentlemen.... Musicians... music... music for Sir Humphrey....

The musicians play an Elizabethan Fanfare. The Europeans cheer exuberantly.... Sir Humphrey bustles his way on the platform, crosses the walkway to join the Ringmaster.... The crowd on the platform comes down both ramps and forms a mob in front of the centre platform....

SIR HUMPHREY: My good fellow... do you mind?
He indicates that he would like the Ringmaster's dais.... The Ringmaster mockingly makes way for him, bowing. Sir Humphrey bows back. On the dais bows to the mob beneath.

SIR HUMPHREY: Thank you, thank you, thank you all very much....

The music fades in a manner suspiciously indicative of a raspberry.

SIR HUMPHREY: *(Aside to Ringmaster)* Would you mind adjusting my cloak, my good fellow? It isn't hanging properly.

RINGMASTER: Do you dress left or right, Sir Humphrey?

SIR HUMPHREY: I beg your pardon?

RINGMASTER: It doesn't matter.... *(The Ringmaster moves to adjust Sir Humphrey's cloak).*

SIR HUMPHREY: A little back from the sword hilt... thank you.

RINGMASTER: Not at all, Sir Humphrey... *(Aside)* No accounting for tastes.

SIR HUMPHREY: Most loyal, trusted, and obedient subjects. I cannot begin to speak of my joy on finally attaining the green shores of this resplendent isle....

RINGMASTER: Doesn't lack imagination, Sir Humphrey. If he thought they'd understand, he'd say the same thing to the gannets on the Funks.

SIR HUMPHREY: It just so happens that I have a speech prepared, a little speech, for this auspicious occasion, an occasion of considerable historical significance as I, and I am sure you, too, in your own peasant ways, are aware. *(Warming up)* An occasion which will ensure my own immortality which you good people will share in some small part for simply being present as I claim this New Found Land for Her Most Gracious Majesty....

MUSICIANS: *Fanfare, ending as before.*

SIR HUMPHREY: It is well known that the striving for immortality is one of the noblest human aspirations, one which, though not necessarily confined to the greatest of men is, perhaps, in them most fully realised.... I myself, spent much time in meditation while upon the savage waters....

RINGMASTER: Sir Humphrey....

SIR HUMPHREY: *(Impervious)* Pondering the astonishing circumstances which fate, in its wisdom, allied to the vision of Almighty God, had chosen me as the principal discoverer and claimant of the New....

RINGMASTER: *(Loudly)* Sir Humphrey....

SIR HUMPHREY: Yes, yes. What is it. I was just getting to the exposition of the argument.

RINGMASTER: You'll have to skip the exposition for now, Sir. Your audience is waiting. Destiny... is waiting.

SIR HUMPHREY: Mmm. Yes. Well, if you put it like that... Destiny... Well. I'll be selective, a few choice phrases, let me see.... *(He rummages through an enormous scroll).* Yes, here we are. After a long journey... I may say, at times, a tedious journey, broken only be the occasional sighting of a whale, or the necessary delays occasioned by avoiding the great cliffs of ice that continually bore down upon us, with the specific intention of crushing us, it seemed; surrounded for the most part by goodly, but inferior fellows, some of whom, I regret to say, had been carried by force from the stews of Bristol and Cork for the purpose of honest seafaring labour, travelling South South West to the 47th parallel we were there afflicted by untimely winds and driven North to an inhospitable place of rock and reef called by some rude fisherman who inhabit there, though God knows why, Bonavista, we were nonetheless finally able to pull back by judicious use of the Labrador current and....

RINGMASTER: *(Shouting)* Sir Humphrey.... That's enough.

SIR HUMPHREY: Oh. Am I going on too long? I can assure you, the populace back home have been know to beg a good sermoniser to keep on, and that after three hours, and the good Sir Walter once harangued Parliament for seven hours and some fourteen minutes and was listened to with great interest throughout. Myself, I once obtained the attention of an audience at a play and....

RINGMASTER: Destiny, Sir, is not an audience. It don't concern itself with details. It provides its own entertainment. And above all, it runs to time.

SIR HUMPHREY: Perhaps then... I should commit this to print. Publish it as a small paper, to be circulated at Court on my return.

RINGMASTER: Publish it anywhere but here, sir. The fish can't read. And those that spends their lives catching 'em isn't about to learn. Now... to business....

SIR HUMPHREY: *(Confused)* Very well... I just thought... I suppose it would be alright in different circumstances.... *(Peering down)* They do look an uncommonly rude lot, I must say, a little unrefined. Oh well... so be it... In the Name of Her Majesty, Queen Elizabeth 1st, by the Grace of God, Queen of All England, Scotland and Ireland, I hereby lay claim to this New Found Land, which claim includes your land, your property, your wives, your daughters....

RINGMASTER: Don't get carried away Sir Humphrey....

SIR HUMPHREY: In fact, anything and everything in perpetuity, and the rights, titles and all privileges attendant thereunto on behalf of Her Most Soveriegn Christian Majesty and her heirs, pray God there be one, and her appointed servant, to wit... me. Long Live the Queen....

One solitary voice echoes from the crowd below... "Long Live the Queen" *(the remainder cheer ironically....)*

RINGMASTER: And now Sir Humphrey... on behalf of the loyal subjects here present, including the Basque, and the Portugee, and the runaway Spaniards, and the odd Turk dotted here and there, as fine a band of lusty whoremongers, murderers, and stockfish men as were ever assembled who, as ye can see, have been deeply affected by your stirring and patriotic sentiments, may I present this slightly salt stained copy of a genuine Wycliffe Bible, salvaged no doubt from the wreck of some great explorer like yourself whose vessel was driven aground on these inhospitable rocks. Its no good to us, anyhow. Even if we could read it, the sentiments wouldn't apply. Now, Sir... observe the inscription....

SIR HUMPHREY: *(Reading)* To whom it may concern... In the house of my fadir ben many dwellings, and if I go to make for you a place oftsoone I schal come and I schal take you to myself.... Well, I am moved. Yes. Moved... *(An audible snuffle....)* moved to tears. I obviously misjudged you all.

RINGMASTER: Oh... I wouldn't say that....*(Aside to the audience).* Pathetic, really, isn't it. The only Admiral... though God knows where he got the title... on a bloody pond somewhere in Europe I suppose... the only Captain of a vessel in history to sit reading on the poop deck as the ship sank beneath him. I wonder what his poor Master and Bosum thought of that, and his "cheer up my lads, we're closer to Heaven than we are to land." Pretty comfort. I suppose that's where Master Shakespeare got the idea for *The Tempest....*

"What care these roarers for the name of King. You are a counsellor. If you can command these elements to silence and work the peace of the present use your authority."

(Pointing at Sir Humphrey) He ran aground in the entrance to St. John's Harbour, too. We had to go out and row him in. It was, ye might say, a characteristic start to four hundred years of misrule. But I'm getting ahead of myself... Sir Humphrey... Sir Humphrey... the Squirrel is waiting.

SIR HUMPHREY: *(Still reading)* ... No man cometh to the fadir, no but by me.... That's a splendid topic for my address to the crew next Sunday, they'll enjoy that.

RINGMASTER: *(Shouting)* Bring on the Squirrel....

SIR HUMPHREY: *(Incensed)* Its not time for that yet. I'm not ready. There's much to be done. I have to make contact with the Indians. Her Majesty expressly wishes to see and have converse with, a Red Indian. Funds have been set aside for a celebration on my return... Mr. Jonson has been asked to devise a splendid masque... The Virgin Queen and the Noble Savage. I have a hold full of gifts. Why, I've even brought Morris Dancers, Musicians to entertain them. Bring them on....

RINGMASTER: The Morris Dancers.... Ho....

SIR HUMPHREY: And wine for the company....

RINGMASTER: Breach a keg, boys.... Wine... wine for Sir Humphrey... wine for everybody....

The crowd beneath cheer and applaud... the musicians strike up a jig...

the furriers run beneath the platforms and emerge with a hobby horse and Morris Dancers costumes. Others roll in a barrel of wine. The cask is breached... goblets are passed hand to hand... one runs up the ramp who hands a glass to the Ringmaster who drinks and hands it on to Sir Humphrey... the crowd form a semi circle between ramps as the dancers, prepared, begin to perform... the musicians play a coarse rendition of the Elizabethan form... sounding as much like the sackbut and flute as possible. The dancing is clumsy, inept, but the crowd, drinking, enjoy it, drinking, cheering them on.... For a few moments, the stage is awash with energy and colour and excitement.... The revelry is stopped by Sir Humphrey who comes down on the European platform and pauses at the top of the ramp....

SIR HUMPHREY: Alright, my lads... well done... well done....
The dancers collapse in a heap... the hobby horse prances for another wild second or two then also collapses, the men beneath crawling out....

SIR HUMPHREY: Now, you all know why we've brought you to the New Found Land. This bright and verdant jewel now set in the crown of Her Gracious Majesty, Good Queen Bess....

1st DANCER: You said there'd be booty....

2nd DANCER: You said there'd be Glory.

1st DANCER: Billows dancing on a peaceful sea.

2nd DANCER: Black eyed maidens....

1st DANCER: Rum oozing from the trees....

SIR HUMPHREY: No, lads, no. What I said, if I can remember... scans well.... Let me see. Ah yes. And you, good yeoman, whose limbs were made in England, show us here the mettle of your pasture. Let us swear that you are worth your breeding, which I doubt not, for there is none of you so mean and base that has not noble lustre in your eyes.

1st DANCER: The noble lustre wore off the first day out.

2nd DANCER: Bloody stupid. Morris dancing in a bog.

1st DANCER: Where's the houses?

2nd DANCER: Where's the people.

1st DANCER: Where's the rum?

2nd DANCER: Where's the trees.

1st DANCER: Where's the wenches?

2nd DANCER: I lost me brother on the way over.

1st DANCER: In a storm.

2nd DANCER: It was all storms....

1st DANCER: Doing his best. Trying to practice.

2nd DANCER: Got to keep a lively leg in our trade.

1st DANCER: Grease all over the deck.

2nd DANCER: Slops everywhere.

1st DANCER: An' he slipped.

Both going to the bottom of the ramp, enlisting the crowd for support during the following....

2nd DANCER: Never stopped, you didn't. *(Crowd react).*

2nd DANCER: Never turned a hair. *(Crowd react).*

1st DANCER: Never once looked back. *(Crowd react).*

1st DANCER: You should 'ave 'eard 'im.

2nd DANCER: *(Mimicking)* Can't tack in this wind, lads.

1st DANCER: *(Mimicking)* Can't reef in this wind lads. *(Crowd react).*

2nd DANCER: And my brother... he was the best dancer in the whole of Somerset.

1st DANCER: Didn't even throw a rope.

2nd DANCER: Read a prayer.... A prayer. Some bloody use.

1st DANCER: Belched a prayer... alright fer the rich.

2nd DANCER: *(Mimicking)* Can't stop, lads.

1st DANCER: *(Mimicking)* He's safe with God, lads.

2nd DANCER: Dancing on the water, hands scrabbling at the water.

1st DANCER: He wor drunk, you said.

2nd DANCER: He wished he were.

They rejoin the crowd, receive expressions of sympathy, drink....

SIR HUMPHREY: My Lads....

The two dancers ignore him.

1st DANCER: He'll dance all the way back, I suppose.

2nd DANCER: Will Betsy wait for'n?

1st DANCER: Never 'as before.

2nd DANCER: No. Never 'as before.

A pause.

2nd DANCER: She won't miss'n.

1st DANCER: Never 'as before.

A pause.

2nd DANCER: A pox on her.

1st DANCER: She'll get a fright.

2nd DANCER: Goin' at it wi' some sailor....

1st DANCER: And 'im going in at the door.

2nd DANCER: Slipping up the stairs....

1st DANCER: Trailing water and seaweed....

2nd DANCER: Cold on the sheets....

1st DANCER: Cold and wet on the sheets....

2nd DANCER: Finish her off, I suppose....

1st DANCER: Enjoying the dance, he'll say....

2nd DANCER: Fishy eyed, looking at her.

1st DANCER: I wouldn't be in Betsy's sheets then.

A pause.

1st DANCER: I wouldn't be in Betsy's sheets then....

2nd DANCER: Better than me brother's....

A pause.

1st DANCER: Warmer, I suppose....

2nd DANCER: Dryer.

1st DANCER: I must look her up....

2nd DANCER: When ye gets back.

1st DANCER: I allus liked Betsy.

2nd DANCER: Everyone liked Betsy....

1st DANCER: A pox on her....

SIR HUMPHREY: That's enough, enough, you mutinous scum. Glory has to be earned. History has to be made. Even you are part of the pattern of destiny. You are going to pacify the heathens, the savages, the natives, the Red Indians....

The crowd cheer.

1st DANCER: What about women?

2nd DANCER: Well... I always got me hobby horse... *(Laughs....)*

1st DANCER: Yes. And I wishes I were at Banbury Cross right now....

SIR HUMPHREY: Silence. The plan is simple. You will be taken to a Bay not far from here and there will be disembarked with provisions, trinkets, such weapons as you may need to fend for yourselves in the possibility of danger, plus a limited quantity of wine to ease communication with the savages. You, *(Pointing at 2nd Dancer)* mounted on your hobby horse, will be drawn into the forest by your comrades to any place where traces of the Red Indians may be found. They will then withdraw to a discreet distance....

2nd DANCER: Christ... he thinks I'm Ulysses.

SIR HUMPHREY: You may sing, if you like, to attract them. They are a simple, gentle people by all accounts, and easily impressed. They are also very rich in furs. Her Majesty is very fond of furs. They are also fond of music. Your singing will bring them out of their caves or wherever it is they live....

1st DANCER: You haven't heard him singing.

SIR HUMPHREY: *(Impervious)* The wooden horse will delight

them. As they gather about you, laughing, poking at you with their arrows....

2nd DANCER: Here....

SIR HUMPHREY: Your commrades, gauging exactly the right moment, may burst from the bush and break into dance, and thus, having established friendly contact, you may drink the wine, exchange the trinkets, and the horse if necessary... for as many furs as you can carry. More than you can carry, for it must be necessary for some of the Red Men to accompany you back to the boat. Once there, you will overpower them, and bring them back to me for examination and education.

1st DANCER: Just like that.

2nd DANCER: Oh... nothing to it.

SIR HUMPHREY: Good day, gentlemen, and God's blessings upon you and your mission. Remember, we are nearer to Heaven at all times....

RINGMASTER: Its not time for that yet, Sir Humphrey, but it won't be long. A pretty good show though. Have you got your Bible.... Good. Think of us during what time you've got left and Bon Voyage.... Ladies and Gentlemen right from the pages of history, your school day hero... Sir Humphrey Gilbert... give him a big hand.... *The crowd applaud... Sir Humphrey, clutching his Bible, walks round and through them, and exits right. The remainder of the Europeans, except for the dancers, move variously up on to their platform....*

RINGMASTER: And, to round off Act Two... the song sung by the legless horseman, left alone at night, in the dark forest, with nothing but wind and stars for company....

Lights fade on Ringmaster.... The European Platform.... a shadow filled circle is created centre... During the song lights rise on mamateek and Indian platform all the Indians move down ramps slowly, gather in a circle around the mamateek....

1st DANCER: *(Sings)* Oh, will I ever be again
On the spring meadows of my home,
with a willing wench
and a round cheese
and a flagon of ale for company?

For I am in a cold land,
where meadow grasses do not grow
and the late song
of the blackbird
stands not between man and the dark fall.

There is a candle in the church,
there is a candle lit for me,
the tallow flakes
on the flagstones..
When the flame dies where shall I buried be?
The Indians begin to make bird calls, animal calls. At first, the dancers, fearful, huddle together, but drinking wine, they relax and begin to play in order to still their fears, taking the cue for their actions from the words of the Indians. The musicians play a soft slow pavane beneath the following....

INDIAN MAN: They were sitting, drinking red wine from glass bottles. Two played with a wooden beast, lumbering and tumbling to the ground and singing, as the wolf sings when the first frost stiffens the pine needles. We wondered... watching them....
A pause... the dancers play... the music continues.

INDIAN WOMAN: They played like children, the red wine staining their beards, but, as the sun fled the skies, the red clouds staining the water, so they grew troubled, and one would drop to his knees and clasp his hands and stare, as a man seeing death stares at the Heavens, and yet another would run to a tall tree and fight up through the branches staring out towards the deep water, and shout in distress to his brothers....
A pause... the dancers try to simulate rest, an uneasy rest. The music continues.... As the Indian Man speaks, the remainder of the Indians go forward to greet the dancers... the actions speak for themselves.

INDIAN MAN: When the mist rose to meet the stars we rose to meet them bringing meat and fire. When they saw we meant no harm, they shouted with joy, the tears wetting their beards. We danced and drank together, and laughed away fear.

INDIAN WOMAN: When you blew into the bottles, it made a sound like an old bear breaking wind....

INDIAN MAN: And when the sun came up, the glass splintered it in all directions....

INDIAN WOMAN: They gave us beads of many colours, and needles, thread and little axes and some cloth.

INDIAN MAN: We gave them furs, beaver and sable and chains made of shells and the dried meat of salmon and deer.

INDIAN WOMAN: This was a happy time.

INDIAN MAN: These were men, like us.

INDIAN WOMAN: They must have died.

INDIAN MAN: They did not come back.

INDIAN WOMAN: Their laughter drowned in the salt water.

INDIAN MAN: Our laughter dying with them.

The music gives way to a harsh, violent, catatonic series of chords....
The two groups depart slowly, moving back to their respective
platforms. Lights fade centre, go up on European platform. The
Indian platform remains in darkness... suddenly, the furriers quartet
push their way to the edge of the platform and repeat their song....

QUARTET: We're going down the Exploits...

We're going down the Exploits...

We're going down the Exploits river....

We're going down the Exploits,

You'd like to go, would you?

Then go you shall, to share the fight

And the glory, too.

Before our guns the foe will fly,

Women, children too.

For we're away at the break of day

To hunt, to hunt the heathens down....

Then here's to the river wide,

And here's to the fray,

And here's to Peyton's merry, merry men

Who won't come back to the Bay again

'Till they've skinned... the enemy's hide....

All the Europeans applaud....

RINGMASTER: Well done, lads... you must admit, they might not
make the Metropolitan Opera but they have enthusiasm, you must
grant them that... they love their work, they love their play, the salt of
the earth....

All the Europeans echo the last line...

COMPANY: The salt of the earth....

RINGMASTER: Listen... we're heading into Act Three, towards the
final curtain, but how's this for a good one. Shanadathit... she was the
last one, the last one of the tribe. Well, there were about seven left when
they got her, including a couple of youngsters, but they were never
seen again. Well, Shanadithit died in captivity, in St. John's,
Newfoundland, on the 6th June, 1829. They knew she was the last of
'em because she'd been in captivity five years by that time. The others,
well, they could have stayed in the woods and starved. Most likely,
though, they tried to come out for a meal of mussels. Very fond of
mussels, they were. Or they might even have had the crazy idea of
getting a pot-head whale. They had this thing about the whale,

worshipped its tail... a fertility symbol or something... and of course if anyone saw 'em....

Well, Shanadithit, she was put down properly, Church of England, a big ceremony, man that is born of woman and all that... and they buried her in the cemetery of the big stone church on the South Side of the City. *(Chokes with laughter)* And one hundred and thirty five years later they pulled it down and covered it with concrete. The last of the Beothuk Indians sleeps beneath a road... Oil trucks thundering up and down... the boys parking for a bottle and a feel on a Saturday night.... That's a good one, eh....

MUSICIAN: *One sustained, sharp catatonic bar of music.*

RINGMASTER: But its not done with yet.... *(The lights begin to fade)*. Not yet. You have to be on guard. The place is haunted. Both sides... tracking through the woods... whispering on the water... waiting for us all to go, I suppose. The fish gone. The stages abandoned. The shores rotting back into the ground, alder and raspberry filling the graveyards. Nothing left then... only the woods and the water, as it has always been... and us and the Beothuks on equal terms after all....

The lights fade on all upper levels... downstage is lit with red glow filtered through bars. A barred effect... figures moving in and out of shadow....

MUSICIAN: *One sustained, sharp catatonic bar....*
The furriers come furtively down the ramp, peering, calling....

1st FURRIER: Mr. Peyton.... Mr. Peyton....

2nd FURRIER: There's tracks here... there's tracks here....

1st FURRIER: Is it time yet?

2nd FURRIER: Not yet.

1st FURRIER: Musket loaded.

2nd FURRIER: Its always loaded.

1st FURRIER: I wouldn't mind if they'd send a different one.

2nd FURRIER: It'd be the same.

1st FURRIER: Yes. It'd be the same.

2nd FURRIER: I've tried not to pull the trigger....

1st FURRIER: I've tried praying....

2nd FURRIER: I've tried to be sorrow....

1st FURRIER: I've tried to be penitence....

2nd FURRIER: I've tried to be love....

1st FURRIER: I've tried to be guilt....

2nd FURRIER: Tried not to pull the trigger....

1st FURRIER: When you don't pull it... it still fires.

2nd FURRIER: That's justice for you.

1st FURRIER: That's God for you.

2nd FURRIER: And now she laughs as she kneels....

1st FURRIER: Doesn't feel it, see... Bitch....

2nd FURRIER: That's God for you.

1st FURRIER: And the milk rushes out....

2nd FURRIER: Round us....

1st FURRIER: Rivers of milk....

2nd FURRIER: Slipping....

1st FURRIER: Falling....

2nd FURRIER: Drowning....

1st FURRIER: And her laughing.

2nd FURRIER: I thought you could only die once.

1st FURRIER: That's God for you....

2nd FURRIER: I didn't mind at first....

1st FURRIER: Me neither.

2nd FURRIER: Cut meself on a rusty knife....

1st FURRIER: Fell through a hole in the ice....

2nd FURRIER: Alright at first... then everything swelled up....

1st FURRIER: Could see the shadows of me mates trying to cut through to me....

2nd FURRIER: Went rotten... rotten meat, crawling....

1st FURRIER: Funny, really, looking up at a pair of boots dying.

2nd FURRIER: Was you surprised?

1st FURRIER: After it happened. The laying down? Not really....

2nd FURRIER: Me neither. A nice ceremony... good pine box, nice and comfortable. Rum fer all hands....

1st FURRIER: Making up stories about yer....

2nd FURRIER: Bit of a song and dance.

1st FURRIER: That was alright....

2nd FURRIER: Yes. That was alright... then....

1st FURRIER: Didn't like it afterwards, though.

2nd FURRIER: The frozen earth....

1st FURRIER: Washed down to the landwash, I was.

2nd FURRIER: Me too. They didn't take enough trouble with the digging....

1st FURRIER: No. Idle buggers. They didn't care....

2nd FURRIER: No. Nobody cared... that's what it was....

1st FURRIER: Bones and bits of fish and refuse....

2nd FURRIER: Bumping on the tide....

1st FURRIER: And then this....

43

2nd FURRIER: I was surprised....

1st FURRIER: All them Indians in the way.

2nd FURRIER: That's God for you....

1st FURRIER: A deer fence round Heaven. Them preachers didn't say nothing about a deer fence....

2nd FURRIER: No. All grass and bloody daffodils, to hear them talk....

1st FURRIER: Chance of a woman or two....

2nd FURRIER: Heavenly moonshine....

1st FURRIER: Accordian and a harp.

2nd FURRIER: Bit of a tune....

1st FURRIER: And the bloody Indians in the way....

2nd FURRIER: A deer fence round Heaven.

1st FURRIER: Thirty eight I killed... you?

2nd FURRIER: Twenty nine.

1st FURRIER: Didn't seem wrong at the time....

2nd FURRIER: Them as didn't do it knew about it....

1st FURRIER: Bloody Pilates....

2nd FURRIER: Always the poor that gets it.

1st FURRIER: That's God for you.

MUSICIAN: *A soft drum roll....*

2nd FURRIER: Here comes the boat....

1st FURRIER: Same old crew.

They are joined by four Europeans from the platform, moving in slow motion.

2nd FURRIER: Same black faces....

1st FURRIER: Muskets loaded....

2nd FURRIER: Gagging at the thought of it....

1st FURRIER: If there's anything worse than drowning once....

2nd FURRIER: Its drowning twice....

1st FURRIER: Drowning forever.

2nd FURRIER: Damned Indians....

1st FURRIER: Aye. Damned Indians....

An Indian woman appears by the mamateek. She laughs softly....

2nd FURRIER: There she is... waiting.

1st FURRIER: Cast off.

2nd FURRIER: Are you ready...?

1st FURRIER: Aye... ready....

The woman, almost floating, flows around them, moves beneath the centre platform....

2nd FURRIER: There she goes, boys....

1st FURRIER: Aye. There she goes....

2nd FURRIER: That's God for you....

1st FURRIER: Indian lover....

In slow motion they move off after the Indian Woman. Peyton stumbles into view, bowed as if carrying a heavy load.

PEYTON: Boys... Boys... wait for me... wait for me....

All the Indians on the platform echo his cry....

INDIANS: Wait for me.... Wait for me....

PEYTON: *(Breathless)* Give us a hand here....

INDIANS: Give us a hand here....

PEYTON: To Hell with you....

INDIANS: To Hell with you....

PEYTON: Jesus.... *(It's a scream....)*

INDIANS: Jesus....

PEYTON: Jesus Christ....

INDIANS: Jesus Christ....

PEYTON: Take this thing off my back....

There is no equivalent answer from the Indians... Buchans... still on platform....

BUCHANS: Reef the topsails....

Peyton turns, stumbles upon the ramp, falls....

PEYTON: Buchans... Lieutenant Buchans....

BUCHANS: Look lively now.... To the yards.... Get a move on....

PEYTON: Buchans... for pity's sake... over here, man... over here....

BUCHANS: Reef her down, now....

PEYTON: Buchans. *(Its a roar of despair....)*

BUCHANS: Sou Sou East....

A voice answers....

VOICE: Sou Sou East it is, sir....

BUCHANS: Steady as she goes....

VOICE: Steady, sir.... *(Repeated as if fading....)* Steady....

PEYTON: Damnable Pig. God... I stink of death. Indian death. Dead Indians... I can't shake it off....

Like a man with a clinging bear on his back he staggers about centre stage, trying to claw at an unseen foe....

The Indians, on the platform.

INDIANS: Dancing, dark, and a white man's head,
birds in the birch pot,
soup for the dead,
snow for the living,

fire for the soul...

and stones in the heart of the healer....

PEYTON: Hey... you... Indians... I have a present for you....

The Indians all begin to move down the ramp chanting....

INDIANS: Dancing, dark and a white man's head. Dancing, dark and a white man's head....

They begin to circle Peyton, chanting.

PEYTON: I have one of your own.... I bring her back to you....Take her.... For the love of suffering Christ, take her....

INDIANS: Dancing, dark and a white man's head, Dancing, dark and a white man's head....

PEYTON: *(Sobbing)* Cut her loose. Let her pass on. Bury her in your secret places. Free me from her....

Indians move around him.

INDIANS: Dancing, dark and a white man's head, Dancing, dark and a white man's head....

PEYTON: *(Screaming)* She's yours. Your flesh. Your body. Your blood. Your bones. Your smell. Take her....

The Indians are still, silent, one detaches himself from the group.

INDIAN: Old man. Come to the water. *(A pause)*. Bring your burden to the water.

PEYTON: Yes. Yes, I will bring her. There you will take her from me.

The Indian leads him gently downstage.

INDIAN: Kneel, old man. What do you see?

PEYTON: *(Kneeling)* Faces.

INDIAN: What faces?

PEYTON: Your faces. Hundreds of them. Swimming up into the light.

INDIAN: Where is your face, old man? White man.

PEYTON: Its not there. *(Shouting)* Its not there.

INDIAN: Bend lower....

PEYTON: *(Almost prostrate, looking)*. Oh God. Oh, dear God....

INDIAN: It is yourself you carry, old man. You have nothing of ours. You have nothing we want. You must pass on with your burden.

PEYTON: Sweet Jesus! Help me....

The Indian rejoins his comrades. They circle Peyton, for the last time and proceed back up the ramp.

INDIANS: Snow for the living,

fire for the soul,

and stones in the heart

of the healer....

and stones in the heart of the healer....

The lights fade to black. Peyton regains the platform via the rear ramp.

MUSICIAN: *A thin, high piping call....*

The lights go up on the mamateek... Shanadithit discovered by it....

SHANADITHIT: I Shanadithit, the last of my people, laboured to free myself of the old mortality, the remembrance of wind and stars,

light, and the limbs of light on the water, light on the limbs of the water....

She breaks down... covers her face with her hands.... From the darkened Indian platform....

NONOSABASUT: *(Soft)* Shanadithit... Shanadithit... It is I, Nonosabasut speaks to you....

DEMASDUIT: Shanadithit.... It is I, Demasduit, speaks to you.

NONOSABASUT: Be strong.

DEMASDUIT: Be true.

SHANADITHIT: I, Shanadithit,

was chosen to be

the book of my people,

was asked to render up

the mysteries of word and faith,

to chant, in a strange tongue

our mythologies....

NONOSABASUT: Do not trust them, Shanadithit.

The wind has heard our singing

and the land folds about us.

Only the water must mirror our passing,

then no harm may befall us....

SHANADITHIT: The lynx kills,

but leaves the carcass to rot,

draining the blood

to fire nerve and sinew.

DEMASDUIT: Shanadithit.

They are fearful

at the loss of wisdom

lest the land rebel,

and the birds and the beasts

and the fish of the seas

rise against them

and come no more....
NONOSABASUT: They are fearful
that the water will grieve for us,
the lakes freeze
as they did before our coming,
and the rivers hide their faces
in the womb of the rock.
SHANADITHIT: Our bones,
abandoned to the North Wind,
are so much driftwood
under the stars.
The ant and the mouse
nest in our loins
and there will be none to grieve.
NONOSABASUT: They are gathering together
in the secret places.
The sky will bring fire
and the wind raise our ashes
to Heaven,
where they will be fashioned anew
into green arrows....
SHANADITHIT: The white men have abandoned
the gun for the soft word
and have given my body back to me.
They woo me with bracelet and braid,
I, Shanadithit,
Princess of lost voices,
Captive of lost ceremony,
clothed in rags.
DEMASDUIT: They will snatch
at a word or a song
to feed to their children.
Fools will gain honour
mouthing our speech,
and empty women,
rattling like bones in a bag,
will steal our clothes.

NONOSABASUT: Shanadithit.... Listen.
DEMASDUIT: Take heed....
SHANADITHIT: *(Covering her ears)* No. No. I shut my ears
but not my heart to you,

for I am Shanadithit,
the last of my people.
It is not good to speak to me
out of the grave.
Though I am dead,
I eat and sleep
and am warmed by kindness.
Though I am dead
I rage, seeing my father's hands
close under the ice,
and the blood of my blood
splattered like berries
on the floor of the forest.
Then would I be
the fog on the water,
the fury of storms,
the fear of the forest
come to seek vengeance.
But I am Shanadithit
of the empty womb.
I am no Goddess,
Can not create my likeness
in the flowers of the field,
nor am I the Father of whales
or the giver of flight to the grey geese....
I am no maker of arrows....

DEMASDUIT: Shanadithit....

NONOSABASUT: Shanadithit....

SHANADITHIT: You have left me six years amongst them, without the blessing of death.

NONOSABASUT: Do not keep us alive in the minds of men.

DEMASDUIT: Or let their dreams arrest our journey....

SHANADITHIT: *(Pleading)* A capful of words, that is all. Memories slipped through the fingers. Pictures for a book.

NONOSABASUT: We were what we were, and nothing changed us, from our coming to our going.

SHANADITHIT: *(At breaking point)* Come for me, Father,
as you did in the pink mornings,
driving the half moon
softly over the still water,
your arms raised

against the rim of the sun's curve,
Your beautiful arms
reaching out to me
from the Rim of the Curve....

She turns... her arms outheld.... A faint light on Demasduit and Nonosabasut... they hold out their arms to her.... As if drawn to them, she ascends the ramp....

DEMASDUIT: Let us pass on....

NONOSABASUT: Let us pass on....

She is received by them, embraced, taken amongst them....

MUSICIAN: *Rich, sonorous, triumphant chords....*

The lights fade on all save the Ringmaster, in spotlight....

RINGMASTER: Listen. Hang on a minute before you all rush off about whatever business sustains you. I've got something to read to you. Its from *The Times* of London. Of course. September 14th, 1829. Its about her and them. An obituary. Very big on obituaries, *The Times*. Only the best people get noticed in there, of course. Funny isn't it. All the crowd that scratched and fought and settled the place... none of them got in. Took an Indian to put Newfoundland on the map. A dead one. Here it is... "Died at St. John's, Newfoundland, on the 6th June last in the 29th year of her age, Shanadithit, supposed to be the last of the Beothuks." *(He folds the paper.)* Supposed to be. She was. We made no mistake about that, did we? Oh well... there you have it... Good night ladies and gentlemen, sweet ladies and gentlemen. God bless you all, and may you all be saved. Don't forget to tell your friends about us. Without your support, we'd never keep a show like this running....

The lights fade... on a prolonged drum roll.

CURTAIN

The Head, Guts and Soundbone Dance.

A controversial play that deals with Newfoundland's future.

CAST

Skipper Pete

Uncle John

Absalom

Aiden)
Lew)   Men of the Village

Child

Wife to Uncle John

The curtain rises on a typical splitting room on a fishing stage. The room rises from the landward side and runs generally to one third of the way out on the stage. At high tide, water runs beneath its whole length. A low tide — the seaward end (rear) still is far enough over the water for guts to be emptied, buckets hauled to wash down. They're low, noisome, dank. The external timbers are skeleton grey. Inside — a luminous green dampness masks the same grey. The largest entrance is at Backstage Centre. When the door opens the platform can be seen — widely spaced pine logs dropping smartly into the sea after a few yards. Inside, Stage Right is a jumble of gear of all kinds, rope, barrels, heaps of netting, buoys. Downstage right is the 2nd entrance, effected by climbing (or jumping) a few feet from the outside up onto the main platform level. At Centre Right is an ancient pot-bellied stove. Backstage Left is the splitting table. Down from that, a couple of salt barrels. The left wall has a ragged window — once a church window, saved from an abandoned church somewhere and put to use by a crude insertion into the room. Low beams spread the rear towards the auditorium. From them, too, hang a variety of implements, pots, grapples, gaffs. Downstage Left is a frame from which hangs a net in the process of completion. At Left Centre a small trap — opened — reveals a drop to the sea. The whole effect must be one of apparent mess and confusion, an immense variety of gear representing man, and fish and the sea in a tottering, near derelict place, and yet also reveal, as we become accustomed to it, an almost fanatical sense of order.

Morning light. A faint sound of the sea. Skipper Pete enters downstage right (does not yet open the door). He stands listening. An explosive screech of gulls. It dies away. He tramps on upstage and disappears. Another explosive screeching of gulls. He opens the door at rear, takes one pace into the room. The door swings back on him. He swears.

SKIPPER PETE: God damn door!

He disappears back through the door. Seizes it from behind, and fastens it — out of sight from the audience. Re-appears in the door frame. Takes one pace inside them turns his back. Looks seaward. Gives a deep grunt — perhaps of satisfaction. Turns — moves a few paces downstage. Pauses. Scratches himself in the crotch. Shakes his head. Unzippers his fly. Turns. Moves back to the doorway. Urinates over the water. Turns. Does up his fly. Gives another grunt of satisfaction. Moves towards the stove. He lifts the stove lid. Puts it to one side. Moves into the jumbled stage right straight to a barrel containing splits. Takes a yaffle. Moves back to stove. Puts the wood in the stove. Moves back up stage right — straight to bottle containing stove oil. Moves back to stove. Pours the oil liberally but carefully onto the wood. Takes back the bottle. Returns to the stove. Extracts a match and throws it in. Stays a moment, waiting to make sure the oil has caught. Grunts again. Replaces the lid. Moves across to net and frame. Picks it up exactly where he left off and begins to knit the net. He stands facing off stage left through the cracked frame of the church window. The light, growing stronger, betrays the presence of sun. He begins to sing fragments of an old ballad.... Looking out as his fingers move amongst the netting....

SKIPPER PETE: At the tender age of sixteen years,
                I had to sail away,
                All on a banking schooner —

He frowns — as if recollecting the words. Smiles. Hums the tune again loudly. Pauses to cough. Then spit. The hands all the time working.

                All on a banking schooner,
                In the morning light of day,
                All on a banking schooner, *(Hums to himself)*
                I stowed my gear away —
                Funny — can't remember it now.

Begins to hum the tune again with concentration... half-way through he's interrupted. Uncle John appears downstage right. Looks up at the sky. Nods at the smoke. Enters the room downstage right. He carries a can slung over his shoulder by a rope. He shuts the door behind him. Pete, still humming, has continued to look out of the window. Uncle John nods in his direction.

UNCLE JOHN: 'Ow do, Skipper.

Skipper Pete nods back without turning his head.

SKIPPER PETE: 'Ow do.

John moves up to the splitting table, swings the can from his shoulder. Puts it squarely in the middle. He comes and stands by the stove, rubbing his hands. A moment's silence.

UNCLE JOHN: Fine morning.

SKIPPER PETE: Seen worse.

UNCLE JOHN: Better than yistiday.

SKIPPER PETE: Not so good as Wednesday afore last.

A pause. John ponders this.

UNCLE JOHN: No. I grant you that. Not as good as Wednesday afore last.

A pause.

UNCLE JOHN: Last Satiday weren't too bad, neither. Got a gallon of berries.

Skipper Pete pauses in his work. Turns and looks at John. Spits thoughtfully.

SKIPPER PETE: Partridge?

UNCLE JOHN: Marsh.

SKIPPER PETE: I allow. Last Satiday weren't too bad.

UNCLE JOHN: Sunday were half decent. Act of God I s'pose. For the Bishop.

Skipper Pete begins at the net again. Spits.

UNCLE JOHN: I saw the Bishop.

Without waiting for any kind of reply he goes into the gloom stage right and emerges with an armful of birch junks. He puts two on the stove. Places the remainder carefully at its feet.

UNCLE JOHN: Did you see the Bishop?

SKIPPER PETE: I didn't bother. No arches.

UNCLE JOHN: No. It's not the same.

SKIPPER PETE: I mind when we used to make 'em along the path 'e'd come. T'ree, four arches... bigger'n old church door, they was. And all the maids wid flowers.

Uncle John goes to door stage right. He throws it open. Looks for a moment. Then from the side of the door where it has been leaning takes a gaff, and props the door open, in such a way it makes two triangles of the entrance. Stands framed in the door.

UNCLE JOHN: He'd come by boat.

No response. A pause. He raises his voice. Skipper Pete is slightly deaf.

UNCLE JOHN: Not the same by boat.

SKIPPER PETE: No. The road's not the same.

UNCLE JOHN: Might a meant something then.

SKIPPER PETE: It did. We made the arches for'n to go under. All the way up the road. Past the houses. It meant something.

UNCLE JOHN: I remember the Bishop up in the boat in his robes. The cross in front of him. The whole place turned out in their best. The harses and sheep driven to top pasture. *(Chuckles)* The hooman sheep to the wharf. *(Chuckles)* Even the pigs clean. Old dogs on chains. *(A pause). (Scornfully)* This one, now. Didn't matter how much shit was on the road. Came by car. *(Indignant. Strides across to Skipper Pete).* A Bishop. Can you imagine that now. Confirmation by car. Where's the God in that I'd like to know.

SKIPPER PETE: No arches. That's what it was. *(He suddenly drops the net). A pause.*

SKIPPER PETE: Time for a mug?

UNCLE JOHN: Aye. *(Half absently)* Aye.

Unhooks ancient black kettle from the beam. Goes back stage right. Dips kettle into barrel of water. Still dripping brings it back to stove. Takes off lid of stove. Places lid to one side. Puts kettle on hole thus exposed. Turns upstage to his can on the splitting table. Extracts the makings for tea. Brings them back to stove. Moves downstage right of door. Hanging on two hooks are four mugs. He brings back two mugs to stove. Stands thinking. Goes back. Gets the other two mugs. Skipper Pete moves left. Selects a barrel. Rolls it towards stove, between the net and the stove. Sits, taking his cap off. Watches John preparing tea. Suddenly sees the other two mugs.

SKIPPER PETE: Where's Absalom?

A pause. John is uncomfortable.

SKIPPER PETE: Should be here.

John busies himself with tea.

SKIPPER PETE: *(Getting angry. He begins to twitch.)* He's never late. Ye are. Often. That woman of yours, I s'pose. Useless as the day ever was. God damnedest child I ever did raise. Glad to be rid of 'er. But Absalom....

UNCLE JOHN: *(Sharply)* He's gone.

SKIPPER PETE: Gone?

UNCLE JOHN: Fishing.

SKIPPER PETE: Fishing? *Half rises, turns to window. A pause.*

UNCLE JOHN: Lard Jesus Christ, where else 'as the bastard got to go.

SKIPPER PETE: But dey's no fish.

UNCLE JOHN: You knows it. I knows it. And he knows it.

SKIPPER PETE: But what's he coddin' about at. *Sits slowly. Puzzled. Pained.*

UNCLE JOHN: *(Bitter)* He 'as dreams. Didn't you know. Dreams of all the fish once. Of the mackerel thicker on the water than moonlight, whispering together. Then 'e 'as to go. Here's your tea. *Hands Skipper Pete his tea. Goes back to stove. Takes kettle off. Puts in two birch junks. Replaces stove lid. Puts kettle on floor. Takes up his own mug. Walks across Skipper Pete to the net. Looks at it thoughtfully. Turns.*

UNCLE JOHN: You've nearly finished.

SKIPPER PETE: Should've finished yesterday.

UNCLE JOHN: Wednesday.

SKIPPER PETE: I allow as how Thursday's alright.

UNCLE JOHN: It's a civil enough day.

SKIPPER PETE: How's the killick?

UNCLE JOHN: Binding to do. That's all.

SKIPPER PETE: Should finish together then.

UNCLE JOHN: Celebrate then, eh? Bit o' shine. Just like the old days.

SKIPPER PETE: Aye. We'll have a time!

UNCLE JOHN: If Absalom's back.

SKIPPER PETE: Can't understand it. We agreed. Next year. New nits. Gear. Four'n us. We'd manage. We'd show the youngsters.

UNCLE JOHN: *(Walks back to stove. Sinks on his haunches)* Aye. They're useless. Bloody great boats they can't handle. Can't hold their liquor. Feared of animals. Like the fella said, wed to music and misery.

SKIPPER PETE: My Absalom. Fishing! Without me! Jesus. The lad'll.... *(Pause)*

UNCLE JOHN: What will he do?

SKIPPER PETE: Nivir did grow up, see. Had to lead'n all the way. That time he fell off the harse on the way out of the woods.

UNCLE JOHN: *(Not without sardonic mirth)* And ye sent him back in didn't ye?" 'Ow many sticks, boy," ye said. "Ninety-five," he said, and it fifteen below and blowing and coming on dark. I remember it now. "Holy Christ," ye roared.... I was just coming from the stage hid then and I heard ye. "Holy Christ. Get back on that damn harse and git another five, or by God, I'll leather you." And him already taller than you.

SKIPPER PETE: Alright for ye to talk now, John. But ye knows ye had to bring 'em up 'ard else they wouldn't survive. Look at 'em now — they's nothing to survive against. I had to do it, John.

UNCLE JOHN: I remember the harse coming back on his own. And it blowing a blizzard then. And us saying we'd better go in and look for'n. And ye saying: "Let the young bugger get here by hisself."*(Chuckles)* I remember it well. "Let the young bugger get here by hisself."

SKIPPER PETE: *(Gets to his feet and glares at John malevolently)* By Jesus, John. Ye watch. I'm not past giving ye a punch in the mout'.

UNCLE JOHN: Don't be so Jesus foolish. Ye'd die of a heart attack. *Pete sits again, breathing heavily. Ancient leader of a savage pack with the instincts still there but the ability in pitiful disrepair.*

UNCLE JOHN: And what'd be the pint. I got nar tooth left anyhow. *(He laughs)* Eh, boy?

Goes across to Skipper Pete and punches him in the shoulder. Skipper

Pete begins to laugh. They laugh together. Cough. Fall out of breath.
Breathe heavily. Suddenly outside — a sudden explosion of gulls.

SKIPPER PETE: Blast dem gulls. Seems as if they do be mocking a man. All the time. Time was....*(Memory fades - comes back)* Time was.... Got me own back on a few of'n, though.

UNCLE JOHN: Aah! Bit of bait on a bobber....

SKIPPER PETE: Down they'd go. Greediest buggers in the sea....

UNCLE JOHN: *(Screeches like a gull — raises his arm).* There they'd be. The hook in their t'roat. *A pause. They both remember meals of seagull.*

SKIPPER PETE: They never seemed to mind it once the wing's was broke.... Tame as chickens, some of'n, an the bread they'd eat.... Get fat as a goose.

UNCLE JOHN: Aye. Seems the law's agin anything a man might do to help hisself to a good meal. *(Gulls screech).* Listen to'n. Got worse since they was protected. *(Gulls screech).* Dam' sight worse.

SKIPPER PETE: Not so bad as the Funks — even now!

UNCLE JOHN: No, not so bad as the Funks.

SKIPPER PETE: I stayed there once all night. For a bet.

UNCLE JOHN: I 'lows I heard that.

SKIPPER PETE: Screeching. All night screeching. Up to me arms in shit.

UNCLE JOHN: *(Laughs).* I'd like to have seen that.
Pete glares. John's laugh dies slowly in his throat. Uncle John moves back towards rear door.

UNCLE JOHN: S'pose I'll go get the killick, then. *No reply from Pete.*

Will I git the killick? *No reply.*

Finished wit yer tay? *No reply.*

Is ye finished wit yer tay, er what?

SKIPPER PETE: Eh?

UNCLE JOHN: Is ye finished wit yer tay? *No answer.*
John crosses. Takes Pete's mug. Goes back and picks up his own. Places both mugs on the hatch. Goes back. Comes back with bucket on the end of a rope. Moves mugs. Lifts hatch. Lowers bucket. Draws up water. Closes hatch. Washes mugs in bucket. Lifts hatch. Pours water away. Is about to close it. Pauses. Decides he wants to urinate. Raises it. Turns back to Pete, facing right. Lowers zip carefully. Is about to commence....

SKIPPER PETE: *(Savagely)* Can't you go outside.

UNCLE JOHN: *(Startled)* Eh?

SKIPPER PETE: Can't you go outside. Always was a dirty bugger. Tanned your arse once on the Labrador for pissin' into the wind. Sprayed all on us. Dirty little bugger, ye was.

UNCLE JOHN: *(Defensive — a child as then)* I were only fourteen then.

SKIPPER PETE: Aye. And you've got the same habits now. There's things better done in private. That's why they're called privates.

UNCLE JOHN: I never called 'em privates. They's in the army.

SKIPPER PETE: What do you know about that, eh? Never was in the army. I was there. Beaumont Hamel. The Somme. You'd never have survived there. Unless I was wid yer. Ye might have stood a chanst then. Privates. What do you know about privates?

UNCLE JOHN: If ye're talking about the same thing I'm talking about I knows as much about 'em as any man. An' right now I want to know what business it is of yours where I pisses, when I pisses and how I pisses.

SKIPPER PETE: I told yer. There's a lot of things done better in private, an' pissin's one of 'em. Dey's places in the world you'd get arrested for doing that. I know. I was there.

UNCLE JOHN: Same sea in't? Sea's a big place.

SKIPPER PETE: Not the pint. I 'low the sea's a big place. Now a man's a small place. You've got to have order. Decency. There 'as to be a way of doing things. A man's way. That's why we're here, isn't it? They's only we left.

Uncle John grumbles and fumbles with his fly. His sense of order has received a setback. He begins to move backstage.

SKIPPER PETE: Hatch.

UNCLE JOHN: *(Turning)* Eh?

SKIPPER PETE: The hatch, then. You've left the hatch open.

UNCLE JOHN: Jesus Christ!

SKIPPER PETE: S'pose a sea hove in. What then?

UNCLE JOHN: *(Turning back disgusted).* Sea. It's like a bloody pond. *(He slams the hatch down).*

SKIPPER PETE: Ye never know. I mind the time — thirty-two was it, or three? Me'n your father was bringing the schooners back from St. John's. Ye was on my boat. Not yet twenty-one, ye were. Ye were safer with me. 'Twas as well I took ye. Yer father an' they was so goddamned drunk after selling the catch they nearly hit the Battery on the way out through the Narrows.

John moves as if to protest but Pete waves him away. John moves stage right and urinates out over the diagonal across door stage right and stays there, a sullen shadow.

SKIPPER PETE: Your father, mind, was a Godless man.

UNCLE JOHN: *(Interrupting)* Ye old hypocrite.

SKIPPER PETE: *(Unmoved)* A man without a decent sense of order. I mind he had a couple o' pigs aboard. And for sport they run 'em up the mainmast in a barrel and let 'n go. Down come the pigs — I saw it, ye didn't. Ye was down below, cooking. The worst cook, I remember, as was ever sent aboard a boat. Smash! All over the boat. Barrel, pigs and all. An' they laughing,drunken fools, the guts flying. I tried to hail 'em. "Look out to your trim, John, b'y. They's weather coming." None of 'em took no heed. Shouted back over the water, "Don't ye mind us Uncle. We's alright. Just knock some fear of God into that boy of mine and leave us be." *(Pete gets up. Goes forestage. Staring out. Reliving the event.)* "Damn fools",I shouted, "Damn fools. Go to Hell, then." *(He's almost dancing with self-satisfaction.)* "Devil's bait", I shouted. "That's what ye'll be afore marnin'." Then the first gust came an' she with all canvas flying ... ripped her mains'l off and she keeled over. An they still laughing and staggering. I'd a prayed then and there, but I reckoned it would 'ave done no good. Aye. *(He stomps slowly back to his seat.)* Saw no more of'n after dark. Wind came on nor'east. Driving snow an' a sea raging like a barren woman. She got fed that night. *(Grim satisfaction)* Not a body ever found. Not a spar.

UNCLE JOHN: *(Turning in from door)* Not even a piece of pig, eh? But Skipper Pete, the Iron Man,came through. Never lost a ship; lost one man in fifty years. Ice and fire, storm and flood — Skipper Pete come through. The legend of the coast! Trips to St. John's. Signed pictures of Joey Smallwood — God knows why, he couldn't stand drinking water! CBC cameras and wet-eared pups praising ye on yer birthday. And what for, eh? What for? *(In a sudden movement almost throws himself face to face with Pete)* It was for ye, wasn't it. Not the ships. Not the men. Ye didn't give a damn for none of it, but for yer own pride.

SKIPPER PETE: I saved you, boy. Don't ye forgit that. More than once. And many another walking the world because o' me.

UNCLE JOHN: *(Anguished).* I would to Christ Jesus ye'd let some of the poor bastards drown. Like me father and they. Drown free. But ye broke 'em, ye did. Like bits of driftwood. Ye saved 'em, alright. But not to stand up. Not to walk the world. Crawl! Ye made 'em crawl. Ye made me crawl. *(Turns back upstage. Turns back. He is crying.)* We should have hung you. But no. I remember me father saying — saying,

"We escaped the rule of others. And exchanged it for the rule of our own kind. No escape boy," he said. "No escape. Except to kill'n or run away agin. And they's nowhere to run." Merciful God!

SKIPPER PETE: *(Roaring)* God is not Merciful. *(He gets up trailing the net after him. Goes to John)* Don't ye ever forgit that. "The Lord is a stronghold to him whose way is upright, but destruction to evildoers." Isn't that what I've just told ye? "He who spares the rod hates his son." Can ye say I didn't love ye?

UNCLE JOHN: I'll give ye back your proverbs." A man's pride will bring him low, but he who is lowly will gain honour." *A pause. Pete turns back, slowly pulling the net together.*

SKIPPER PETE: Ye can't say I didn't teach ye, neither.

UNCLE JOHN: *(Coming after him)* But what does it mean? What does it mean? *(Grips him by the shoulders and turns him. They face each other. Still in command, Pete throws John's hands off. They stand facing each other.)*

SKIPPER PETE: It doesn't matter what it means. It's enough that it's there.

UNCLE JOHN: It's not enough. Ye use it when it's convenient. Like people. But I knows ye well enough. When ye wants to cuss ye cusses. And when ye wanted a woman ye took'n. And when ye wanted a drink ye got drunk like the rest of us.

SKIPPER PETE: No. Ye damn fool. I did those things when I had to.

UNCLE JOHN: When ye had to! Why — you're making an excuse! An excuse!

SKIPPER PETE: No. It was to show ye it was possible for a man to fall and rise. *(Suddenly chuckles)* An it kept ye all guessing. *Goes back to his seat.*

UNCLE JOHN: *(A light dawning)* So that's it. When ye'd druv us to the point o' mutiny ye'd always do something — human. You bastard.

SKIPPER PETE: It had to be done! Ye agreed yourself. To survive. I did what was best. An they was order to it. Like ye said. About the Bishop. And the youngsters. They's got no arches now, ye see. Just space. And they flop about like broken birds, hither and yon, lost. I made an arch for ye. Aye —an' I wasn't the only one either. They was others.

UNCLE JOHN: Arch! 'Twas a bloody prison. *(Confused)* Dey's something there, though. *(Walks forward right)*. Something. Can't quite put me finger to it. Is it because I'm what I am that they is what they is. Because o' ye and them.

SKIPPER PETE: It's all of it. It's ye and the Govermint, wid its eddication and its handouts, and the women snivelling after hot air stoves and 'lectric ovens and motor cars and Bishops goin' from altar to altar and seein' nothing between.

UNCLE JOHN: *(Unhearing)* They was either hypocritical, God-driven old tyrants like ye, or wild men like me fader, who cursed God and man and the sea until one o' the three took'n. *(A pause).*

SKIPPER PETE: *(Sighs)* We'se old men now, me son. No pint in us fretting now. Just do what we has to do. That's all they is. Relive the good times. *(A pause).* They was good times. *(John does not answer).* They was good times. *(John is staring painfully out)* Canvas, salt-stiff, cracking in the wind. Fish in their t'ousands. The voyage home wid a fair wind and the holds full. Walking thru the skinny clerks o' St. John's. They feared to look at'n. Aye, they was good times.

UNCLE JOHN: Were they? *(A pace towards Pete)* I need to know, Pete. God help me, I don't know myself. Was they good times? *Pete looks at him. Then down at the net in his hands.*

SKIPPER PETE: I'll finish me net now, son. It's time. *This is said with an air of finality. John pauses a moment, indecisive. Then moves backstage area. Exits onto stage head.*

SKIPPER PETE: *(Singing-humming)*
> Eternal father strong to save
> Whose arm does bind the restless wave.
> *Pauses — puzzled. To himself.*

That's no good fer today. Today's fer celebratin'. The end of the voyage. The journey. *(Hums again).*
> At the tender age of sixteen years,
> I had to sail away,
> All on a banking schooner,
> In the morning light of day.

A woman's voice outside.

WOMAN: John. John.

SKIPPER PETE: *(Looks up sharply. Cocks his head, spits with disgust).* Get in anywhere, they will.

John staggers back through Back Stage door carrying a hugh killick. Places it right centre.

WOMAN: *(Off)* John. Are ye there?

SKIPPER PETE: Don't let that in 'ere.

UNCLE JOHN: 'Tis yer own daughter. *(Bitter)* Remember?

SKIPPER PETE: Kin be the Divil's for all I know. Jest don't let it in here.

The woman appears in Down Stage right doorway.

WOMAN: There you are.

SKIPPER PETE: *(Laughing without mirth)* Go to her, boy. Go to her. *(Mimics)* John. John.

UNCLE JOHN: *(Angry)*. Ye mind, Skipper. Ye mind. She wouldn't 'a come unless it was important.

Pete spits emphatically once more. John crosses to his wife. She's still standing outside the door.

WIFE: I jist wanted to know, John, if ye was coming to Aunt Alice's funeral. It's at three o'clock.

UNCLE JOHN: *(Uncertain)*. Oh, aye. I'd forgotten. We was finishing up, ye see. I s'pose we'd better go, then. *Turns to Pete.* Will we be done by three, Skipper? *(Pete doesn't bother to answer. John takes a pace towards him.)*

SKIPPER PETE: When did she die?

Wife climbs across entrance, and goes right of John.

WIFE: Last night, poor soul. And her as frail as a bird. "Put another quilt on me, for the Lard Jesus sake," she said, not meaning it blasphemous, mind, "For I'm so thin I'm sure I'll fly to Heaven afore me times up." And she laughed then, ye know — just like a poor sick chicken the sound was, a little whispering in the throat, and then she closed her...

SKIPPER PETE: *(Abruptly)* Which cemetery?

UNCLE JOHN: *(Anxious to prevent his wife getting into full flow again)* That'd be the Pentecostal, wouldn't it, maid? Alice and they was all Pentecostal.

SKIPPER PETE: *(As if unhearing)* What cemetery did ye say?

UNCLE JOHN: *(Shouting)* Pentecostal. She's to be put down in the Pentecostal.

SKIPPER PETE: I'll not be going. Never been to a Pentecostal service in me life an I'm too old to start that foolishness now.

WIFE: She was kin, father. Ye should be ashamed of yerself. And she did many a good turn for our poor mother, God rest her soul.

SKIPPER PETE: *(Suddenly raging)* Ah, to the Divil with the lot o' ye. What she did fer yer mother on this earth might help her in the next and I wish her good luck wi' her good deeds. But she did nothing for me, and she's a Pentecost. And I'll not be going to any arm-raising mumbo jumbo like that. *(As an afterthought)* Not while I'm alive, anyways.

WIFE: Ye haven't changed. *(She pushes past John and crosses to Pete)* Not one bit, father. Only one breath away from God or the Devil hisself and still as spiny as a whore's egg.

SKIPPER PETE: Mind yer place, girl. Ye're in my house and don't forgit it.

WIFE: *(Hurling across stage right)* House is it? *(Laughs)* A house. Oh sure, 'tis where ye spend time making fools of yourselves, the two of ye. Coiling and uncoiling the same rope day after day. Knitting nets you'll never use. Making killicks. And they's only fit now to make ornaments in the homes of the stuck-up in St. John's and upalong. Talking about things that once were and will never be again, Thank God. *(She is flushed and angry. Storms over to the killick and with one heave pushes it over.)*

UNCLE JOHN: That's enough, maid. Ye've no right to be saying those things.

WIFE: Enough! Oh, 'tis enough, alright. I saw ye with the can on yistiday. Time for another celebration, is it? A drunk at the end of the voyage and ye nivir moving from the stage hid from one day — no year — to the next. An' poor, simple Absalom the only one can stand upright in a boat. What'll the catch be today boys? Three — four fish!

UNCLE JOHN: That's enough, woman. 'Tis no business of yours. We don't harm no one.

WIFE: Just ye, John. *(Softening, putting her hand on his arm)* Can't ye see? That's the way he holds onto ye, now. Just like it used to be. Smash yer face in if he caught ye with a drink on the voyage, and then encourage you to riot yer last cent away at the end of it, so ye had to go back. He's still doin' it, John. And ye should be at home now, on the daybed, or out on the bridge. With a nice cup of tea and a few squares I'd make ye. Living comfortable. Talking to yer neighbours. Waiting to see yer grandchildren.

Pete gets up. The conversation has taken a dangerous turn. He points his stick at her.

SKIPPER PETE: I nivir wanted ye in my house. When ye were born. And I still don't want ye. Get out. *(He moves as if to strike her with his stick but she is unflinching, unafraid. Scornful.)*

UNCLE JOHN: Come on, maid. Come on out, now. I'll think about the funeral. *(He takes her by the arm as if to propel her to the door)*

WIFE: Get your foolish hands off me. I'll find me own way to the door. Aye, and home. And to me Maker when the time comes. *(She moves to the door. Turns back)* Don't forgit yer supper will be waiting. And the television ye're ashamed to tell him ye watch. And the electric blanket the doctor told ye to get to keep your arthritic bones from paining at nights. *(Makes one last desperate effort)* For the love of

God, John. Leave off this foolishness and come home. *John pauses, uncertain.*

SKIPPER PETE: Go home, John, for the Lard Jesus sake. Go home. I'll celebrate the end of the voyage by meself.

UNCLE JOHN: I'll be along bye and bye, now, Maid.

WIFE: An' I knows when that'll be. *(Almost in tears)* They's times, so they is, when I wishes you'd fall into the water to be bait fer the connors and the tansies. If they's anything more foolish than a drunken young man 'tis a drunken old one. And if theys anything more foolish than a fine young man thinking he can make a living from the sea, 'tis an old man who can't stop lying to himself about the living he used to make. *She turns, exits, pausing on the other side of the barrier to say...* I 'll say a prayer at the graveside for ye, father. But I doubt it'll do any good.

We hear her as she walks back along the rim of the stage and down the steps.

A pause.

SKIPPER PETE: *(Savage)* I told ye not to let her in.

UNCLE JOHN: *(Defensive)*She's your daughter.

SKIPPER PETE: Useless bitch. Always was. Can't understand why ye married her.

UNCLE JOHN: *(Angrily raising the killick and dragging it towards his seat)* Ye was happy enough fer it to happen at the time.

SKIPPER PETE: *(Laughs)* Thought I'd get rid of both of ye at once. Killing two birds with one slingshot.

UNCLE JOHN: No. No. That's not it. *(He stumps up stage right. Finds some heavy twine. Comes back and begins to fasten the four ends together)* Ye thought.... *(viciously tightening the rope and punctuating his words with the actions)* Ye thought that... with two of your responsibilities under one roof... that it'd be easier to bend'n.

SKIPPER PETE: *(Is enjoying himself. Is enjoying John's anger)* John! John! When your father was drownded, I took ye fer me own. Treated ye just like me own sons.

UNCLE JOHN: *(Bitter)* Aye. That's true enough.

SKIPPER PETE: Now they's you and Absalom. And me. That's all they is left of all of us. And I thought, if ye married me daughter, ye might be able to shut her blather long enough to give me a grandson, even two, maybe.

UNCLE JOHN: *(Stung)* There you goes again. Give you a grandson. Not me. Not for her and me. No. D'ye know what ye did? Ye came between us even there, that's what ye did. It was like.... *(He struggles for words — feelings. Desperation)* I'd be lying atop her and I'd hear your voice. Roaring. "Give it to her, son. Give it to her. Don't stop now. Don't give up." And she felt the same. We had to stop.

SKIPPER PETE: *(Still goading)* Two daughters. And ye had to stop! What a man!

UNCLE JOHN: There was no love in it. Ye killed it. In her. In me.

SKIPPER PETE: *(Mock rage)* What's love got to do with having sons. They's necessary. To make things continue as they were. To...

UNCLE JOHN: Then why in Jesus name didn't ye knock her up yerself.

A shocked pause. John is shocked at himself. Pete, however, is not.

SKIPPER PETE: That's blasphemy, son. The real kind. Not a man's kind.

UNCLE JOHN: *(Tormented)* God damn it. I didn't mean it. Not that way. *(Desperate)* Ye knows I never meant it that way.

SKIPPER PETE: What way did ye mean it?

UNCLE JOHN: *(Raging around like a tormented animal, touching something here, throwing rope down there, spinning a barrel across the floor)* This is it, isn't it? This is us, God damn it, this is the answer to the sum the teacher could never knock into me stupid skull. And I hates it. I hates it. *(Throws more gear about.)* But I don't understand anything else. It's too late. *(A pause. He goes and slumps by the killick, his head in his hands.)*

SKIPPER PETE: *(Rises. Crosses to him. Puts a hand on his shoulder. Goes backstage, speaks out of the gloom)* Ye do understand, son. We understand. The old way. The only way. The proper way to do things. Greet the day at cockcrow. The sea, no matter the weather. Stack the gear. Mend the nets. Make the killick. Keep the store in order. They's nothing without it. *(A moment of insight)* The new ways is for new people, that's all. We don't want their sympathy, and I don't give a damn if anyone understands it or not. It's just the way things always was. *(Softly)* When fish was t'ousands, that was the time. Sea and wind howling like the Devil after a man's soul but the traps was out and the fish waiting. *(Pete comes down and takes John by the arm and raises him up)* Look, boy. Look. *(He turns him round and they stand facing out through the church window over the sea.)* The sun's on the water. Just like it was. Days like this when we've given her every stitch of canvas and foamed down the sound — the water alive with boats about us all rushing to git to the grounds first. Good men, John, b'y. Good men. But they's gone. And their boats gone wid'n. And the land gone wid'n, too. The fences broken. The trees marching back over the hayfields.

There is a noise outside. A shouting. A child's voice.

CHILD: Somebody, quick! Jimmy Fogarty's fallen off the wharf!

SKIPPER PETE: *(Unhearing)* People kin laugh at us, John, b'y. But we know what we is.

CHILD: *(Offstage)* Help! Quick, somebody! *(Appears in doorway stage right. Rushes in)* Uncle John! Uncle Pete! Jimmy Fogarty's fallen off the wharf fishin' for connors and he can't swim! He's drowning!

SKIPPER PETE: *(He and John still facing out. Pete with his arm gripped tightly on John's. They don't turn round. The child is behind them).* I minds when young Amos fell overboard from his father's schooner on the Labrador. Remember that, John? Wind a bit fresh. They wasn't watching the sail. Jibed a bit sudden and took him straight over the side into a school of dogfish.

UNCLE JOHN: Aye. I remember that, alright.

CHILD: *(Tugging at them from behind)* Uncle John! Uncle Pete! Please come quick! Jimmy's drowning!

UNCLE JOHN: Stripped clean in ten minutes. Took three of us to hold his father down from going in after him.

SKIPPER PETE: Aye. No pint in two of 'em feeding they devils.

CHILD: *(As any child ignored by adults persistently. Less forcefully)* Jimmy Fogarty's in the water. *(They ignore him. The child rushes off. His cries for help fading in the distance)*

SKIPPER PETE: Every time they'd haul a dogfish in the nit after that he'd hack it to pieces.

UNCLE JOHN: Aye. Like a wild man. Or he'd cut his belly open just enough for the blood to show, then fling it back overboard and watch his brothers eat'n alive.

A pause. There's a commotion outside which continues as Pete comes down slowly to his net. John to his killick. They begin to finish their work.

SKIPPER PETE: We shouldn't be too long at it, now.

UNCLE JOHN: Not long. *(He wrestles with the twine)*

SKIPPER PETE: Absalom's not so foolish he'd stay out all day?

UNCLE JOHN: I 'lows he'll come in directly, now, when he's caught something.

SKIPPER PETE: Then we'll have our own Thanksgiving.

UNCLE JOHN: *(Laughs, without mirth)* Well. We'm alive. We can give thanks for that.

The noise outside is punctuated by a long high-pitched woman's howl.... An outburst of voices which dies away. Pete gets up and looks out of the window. Turns.

SKIPPER PETE: I 'low that the day is as civil as Wednesday afore last.

UNCLE JOHN: I allow that it is. *(Nods. Smiles)* I 'low 'tis.

He works on in silence as

BLACKOUT

ACT TWO

The finished net is looped and draped from the beams stage left. The killick, finished, is now down-stage left. Pete and John are sitting on two barrels on either side of the stove. In front of them another, smaller barrel on which rests three glasses and the jug of shine. As the curtain opens they are sitting, staring ahead, saying nothing. In the distance a bell begins to toll. John, after a moment listening, gets up slowly, goes to window left and stands looking out.

UNCLE JOHN: That's the bell for Aunt Alice. *(No response)* Quite a crowd too. They's Faheys. They's Catholic. Culls. They's Anglican. An' all the Pentecosts, o' course. Looks like it's goin' to be one of they mixed service everyone keeps on about. *(A snort from Pete)*

SKIPPER PETE: That's easy for funerals.

John turns from the window, surprised.

UNCLE JOHN: Eh?

SKIPPER PETE: Mixed funerals. They's easy. Don't mean nothing when the party's dead.Christenings now — that's different.

UNCLE JOHN: How is it different?

SKIPPER PETE: You never heard tell of the Pope attending a mixed christening, now, have you.

UNCLE JOHN: *(Puzzled)* No — I can't say that I have.

SKIPPER PETE: Well. Until he do I'll stick to what I know. I thought I'd taught you that.

The bell is still tolling. John turns his head back and looks out. He says — with a trace of irony.

UNCLE JOHN: Ye taught me so much, Skipper. I 'lows it's difficult to remember all of it.

SKIPPER PETE: *(Unaware)* Never change a habit or an opinion until someone proves there's a better one.

UNCLE JOHN: You and the Pope 'as got something in common after all then, Skipper....

Pete, surprised, is about to query this when there is the unmistakable sound of a four horse power Acadia.

SKIPPER PETE: Listen, John. Listen.

Still it can be heard — amongst the bells.

SKIPPER PETE: Damn those bells. Enough to jangle the wits from the living.

The bells suddenly stop. The Acadia has the world of sound to itself.

SKIPPER PETE: It's Absalom. Absalom, I'll be bound.

John, too, is excited. He rushes backstage to the stage head door. Shouts back.

UNCLE JOHN: It's him. It is Absalom.

SKIPPER PETE: Any fish?

UNCLE JOHN: What?

SKIPPER PETE: Any fish?

UNCLE JOHN: Can't tell from here.

SKIPPER PETE: Then ask him, ye fool.

John cups his hands.

UNCLE JOHN: Absalom. Hey, Absalom. Any fish?

The sound of the engine is quite close now.

UNCLE JOHN: Fish, boy. Any fish? *(A pause)* Skipper. He's holden'n up. He's got — one, two — my God, he's got six. And they's big 'uns.

SKIPPER PETE: That's my Absalom. Six, eh? A harvest. John, me son. The pan....

John scuttles to the table. Gets the pan. Brings it reverently down to the stove. Puts it on. Goes down right. Fetches bucket. Lifts hatch. Lowers bucket. Fetches up water. Puts bucket down. Lowers hatch. Pours some water from the bucket into the pan. Pauses.

UNCLE JOHN: Skipper. The table.

SKIPPER PETE: *(Lost in reverie)* 1913, now, that was the year. 900 quintals, boat loaded until she was awash. Weather perfect. The sea like glass. The icebergs rearing up and folding in the sun. Lost a man that trip — that's all. Tommy Burns, from Greenspond. Fell overboard. Drunk. A single man, though, not as if he'd a family to keep. We divided his share among the rest of us.

UNCLE JOHN: Skipper. The table!

SKIPPER PETE: Eh? Oh, aye. The table.

He gets up slowly and goes back to John. With difficulty they raise the table and bring it down right centre. The gear is left on it. John unhooks oilskins from right wall, hands them to Pete, who begins to draw them on. John sets three plates, knife and fork and places them up stage left. Busies himself sharpening the splitting knife. Just as he's done this the sound of the motor stops. For a minute only the sound of the sea, and the occasional gull cry. Pete turns on his barrel and stares at the doorway. John — standing — does the same thing. Absalom stands framed in the stage head door, six fish hanging from a hook in his huge hand. He is gaunt and bent. Despite the age of Pete and John, we've been expecting, because of the conversation, someone much younger. But he is, of course, sixty, or near to it. He has still, however, the face of a child — a characteristic of some aspects of retardation. He speaks slowly, with difficulty, and has trouble looking his father in the face.

ABSALOM: I got some fish, father.

SKIPPER PETE: Good boy. That's a good boy. Bring them here, Absalom. Bring them here, me son.

ABSALOM: I forgot to tell you I was going fishing, father.

SKIPPER PETE: That don't matter now, boy. Bring them here. *Absalom advances cautiously into the room towards the table. Places the fish upon it.*

ABSALOM:You see, father, the sun was shining.

SKIPPER PETE: *(His eyes gloating over the fish)* That's alright, boy. Alright.

ABSALOM: And I had a dream of fishes, father. Just like you talk about and I can never remember. The sea was all fish, father. There was no water, hardly.

SKIPPER PETE: *(Impatient)* It doesn't matter, son. Dreams don't matter. Fish — that's all that matters.

ABSALOM: *(Persistent, like a child)* But you were in the dream, father.

Pete takes a splitting knife from his trousers and a small sharpening stone. He begins to sharpen it with slow, deliberate actions, ignoring Absalom.

ABSALOM: I told ye. The sea wasn't the sea. It was fish. And ye were there, picking them up in your hands. Your hands. I couldn't tell what was fish and what was your hands. *(Agitated)* I had to go, ye see, father. On account of yer hands.

UNCLE JOHN: I told him, Absalom. And it was the right day to go. A good day to go. The one day — *(He eyes Pete furtively, slides round table to barrel with mugs and shine on it. Pete, humming now, still*

70

sharpening knife. John pours. He whispers.

UNCLE JOHN: Drink, Absalom?

Absalom reaches for the mug eagerly, both lift mugs to their lips when...

SKIPPER PETE: Nobody drinks. Not yet.

Like guilty school boys, both pause.

SKIPPER PETE: The fish, first.

The two hold a tableau, mugs to mouth, almost. Put mugs down. Move to table. Pete splits, guts and removes the sound bones of the fish. Absalom, at a word from John, draws water. With a swish of his hand he sweeps the offal to the floor. John guts remainder of fish, passes to Pete who splits them. John takes the fish to the bucket still containing salt water and rinses them.

SKIPPER PETE: Water ready?

UNCLE JOHN: She's bilin'.

SKIPPER PETE: Put this one in the pot. Keep the rest for another day.

John puts the fish into the pan on the stove. He takes the remaining three backstage to a salt barrel. Lifts the lid, drops the fish in. Replaces the lid. Absalom clears off the knives. Pete removes oilskins. John comes down, rinses his hands in the bloody water in the bucket, then joins Pete and Absalom who have moved right to drinks. The two look at him, expectantly. Pete pours himself a mug of shine, raises his glass to his lips. The other two, with audible sighs of relief, do the same, when...

SKIPPER PETE: No.

In pained disbelief they watch Pete lower his mug.

SKIPPER PETE: The table first. John. Absalom.

With reluctance, they lower their mugs. John opens the trap. Throws down the bloody water. Lowers the bucket. Raises it. Swills down the table, wiping the remnants away with his hand. Absalom fetches a mop. Sweeps water and offal towards the trap. John raises bucket again, washing down floor. The operation complete, the trap is lowered. John and Absalom return to the drinking barrel. They pause — ancient fishing soldiers awaiting orders.

SKIPPER PETE: Now. We drink.

Mugs are raised, tilted, drained. A moment of reverential silence.

SKIPPER PETE: Well, b'ys.

UNCLE JOHN: Well.

ABSALOM: *(After a pause)* Well.

SKIPPER PETE: The end of the voyage.

UNCLE JOHN: The end of the voyage.

SKIPPER PETE: A drink.

John once again pours three mugs of shine. Once again the three mugs are tipped slowly, deliberately, and drained. Moment of silence and intense inner satisfaction.

SKIPPER PETE: Well, b'ys, what's the news?

A pause.

ABSALOM: Father. I heard Aunt Alice died.

SKIPPER PETE: That's not news. That's history.

A pause.

UNCLE JOHN: They's catching plenty of herring in Placentia Bay.

SKIPPER PETE: They are?

UNCLE JOHN: I heard it on the news. The big boats. They's all there, catching herring.

SKIPPER PETE: Why ain't there none here, then?

UNCLE JOHN: I don't know. *(The drink has made him more belligerent)* How the hell do I know. You always ask foolish questions. All I know is they's herring in Placentia Bay.

SKIPPER PETE: That'll be the last place.

UNCLE JOHN: I 'low it will.

SKIPPER PETE: None after that. They stripped her clean, b'ys.

ABSALOM: Can we take the boat, father? Can we catch herring in Placentia Bay?

SKIPPER PETE: *(Roaring)* It's four hundred miles away, boy. *(Laughs)* And if they heard ye was coming they'd all swim away. Absalom, the fisherman.

UNCLE JOHN: He got today's fish. And they isn't any fish. Give the boy credit.

SKIPPER PETE: I'll give him credit. I taught him all he knew. If there was just one fish left in the ocean he should be able to find it. That's what I taught ye. And them damn politicians, and their stupid industries; and that damned Ottawa, letting every bloody foreigner in the world drag the beds clean — they don't know nothing.

UNCLE JOHN: Ye should have taught them, too. To spill their guts out into the ocean.

SKIPPER PETE: *(Unmoved)* Relief. *(Spits)* Welfare. Education. What was wrong with these, eh? *(Holds up hands)* What was wrong with these?

UNCLE JOHN: But ye knows, Skipper — they's no fish now. We're playing a game, that's all. A death game. The woman's right.

SKIPPER PETE: *(Suddenly strikes John — he stumbles and falls)* It's not a game. Ye cursed blind fool. We gits ready fer the fish year after year, that's all. And we waits. And out there, they knows we're waiting. And one day, they'll come back, in their t'ousands, when all the boats has gone away, and nobody thinks they's anymore. They's waiting for the old days like we is. When the trap and the handline and the jigger was something they understood and we understood. We took what we could get. They knew us, and we knew they, and they bred faster than we could take them. They bred enemies, too, theirs and ours. *(John rises slowly, holding his head)* We understand each other — the sea, and the cod, and the dog fish, and the sculpin and the shark and the whale. They knew us and we knew they. And if we keep ready, and we keep waiting, they'll come again. We can't give up on 'em. We can't give up on ourselves. I nivir give up on ye. *Pete is nearly in tears. He stumbles and puts an arm round each shoulder — John's and Absalom's)*

UNCLE JOHN: Christ. Ye're mad, Skipper. Mad. I knew it all along. But God help me, I prayed ye might be right. *(He, too, in tears)* I still prays. I looks out over the sea, and it looks the same, but it isn't. It's dead. The hulks rotting on the shore. Maybe, maybe we should give it all up, eh? Should turn our backs on this and lock the door and nivir come back no more. Die decent. We got our memories, Skipper. No-one can take them away.

SKIPPER PETE: Memories ain't no good unless you can see someone else working out the same ones.

ABSALOM: Father. Father...when are we going into St. John's? *A pause.*

UNCLE JOHN: Ye see. Six fish. When are we going into St. John's? Jesus Christ — it's funny. If it wasn't Absalom, it'd be funny.

SKIPPER PETE: They's nothing funny about it. The boy just remembers, that's all.

UNCLE JOHN: Oh, yis. We'll take the schooner now. We'll go down through the sound out into the bay and sail right round to St. John's and there we'll sell our season's catch. Six fish. It's alright to get drunk here, because this is us. And I don't mind. But I'm dying, Skipper. And so is ye. And the trouble is the god damn place has died afore us. We can't git that out of our guts, can we?
A pause.

SKIPPER PETE: Drink. *(He pours three more mugs. Once again they drain the cups. All are tangibly drunk.)*

SKIPPER PETE: *(As if talking to a child)* Ye remembers, sometimes ye'd plant potatoes in a dry year. No rain. And the tops burnt before they had a chance to flower?

UNCLE JOHN: Aye, I can remember that.

SKIPPER PETE: Did that stop ye planting next year?

UNCLE JOHN: 'Course not. Every year's different.

SKIPPER PETE: *(Triumphant)* There ye are. And suppose we didn't mend nets, and make killicks, and then come a year when even we could take to the boat and haul fish out like in the good old days. Suppose we wasn't ready then. And they's no young men to go out and get their hands dirty. What then?

UNCLE JOHN: Skipper. Ye haven't been in the boat for two years, now. They's only Absalom got the strength in his arm to heave the engine over. Every year the same, roll her down, tie her to the collar, and then pukin' 'cos you can't crawl aboard'n. Why you was blarin' at him 'cos he went out on his own.

SKIPPER PETE: I don't care. We've got to be ready. I got one more trip to make. I don't know when. But I got one more trip to make. *He slumps into the chair. For a moment he looks tired and defeated. John makes a move towards him — half puts out a hand. Draws it back. Turns. Pours out three more mugs of shine. Looks at Absalom. Looks at Pete. Conspicuously puts both the other mugs together but makes no move to offer them to anyone. Picks up his own glass with great care. Walks down front right. Raises glass to his lips, lowers it. Belches with satisfaction. Looks round slyly towards Pete. Looks front. Raises mug and drains it. Walks back, a little unsteadily towards the table. Thumps the mug down hard. Absalom jumps like a rabbit. No response from Pete. Slowly and deliberately goes right. Unzips his fly, and stands as if about to urinate.*

SKIPPER PETE: *(Without raising his head)* I told ye.... I told ye before. Dirty bugger.

John sighs with relief. Doesn't turn yet.

SKIPPER PETE: *(Raising his head and glowering malevolently)* Never learn, will ye? Only yistiday I told ye.

UNCLE JOHN: Today. *(With satisfaction)* It was today.

SKIPPER PETE: *(Roaring)* Today. Yistiday. What's the difference?

Absalom picks up his father's mug and proffers it gingerly. After a moment, Pete grabs it and drinks.

SKIPPER PETE: *(To Absalom)* And I told ye. No more fishin' on yer own. Ye wait fer me.

John lets out a sharp burst of laughter. Absalom nods in agreement. Picks up mug. Drinks. There is a general silence. All three are waiting.

SKIPPER PETE: Well. *(No response) (To John)* Are you going to stand there with yer cock out all day?

UNCLE JOHN: It's not out. *(A pause)* I nivir got'n out. *(A pause)* I couldn't find'n. *(Begins to laugh. Pete digests this but if the information means anything, doesn't show it. John moves unsteadily across left and looks out of the window.)*

UNCLE JOHN: They's lots of fun out there. Big crowd. Half the place on the wharf. *(A pause)* Looks as if they's fishing for something. That's odd now.

He turns, and there's a moment of uncertainty as if trying to recollect something. He shakes the thought away. Staggers back down to the table. Discovers that his fly is unzipped. Zips it up, catching his finger in the process. Curses....

UNCLE JOHN: *(To Pete)* I bet you can't find it, neither. I bet it's all covered with kelp and barnacles. *(Laughs. Pours another drink.) Absalom, after having been perfectly still throughout this interchange, suddenly falls against the table. Straightens himself in slow motion.*

ABSALOM: Father. *(He speaks with some difficulty)* Father. Aren't ye going to sing, father.

UNCLE JOHN: Oh Absalom, my son. Absalom. Absalom. *(going to him and putting his arm round his neck)* What did he sing to ye, boy. When ye was in the cradle. Rocking ye to and fro in his clammy hands. *(He sings in a mutilated voice)* I sailed out to the Labrador When I was but thirteen... *(Pause)* I never could sing. And now I can't find it, neither. *(A pause)* Yer father, now. Like a god damn foghorn. Could hear him right across the Bay. *(Sings again)* I sailed out to the Labrador When I was but thirteen... Me mother wept... Me mother wept.... Aw to hell wi' it.

Lets go of Absalom and collapses heavily on the bench. Suddenly Pete begins to sing.

SKIPPER PETE: I went out to the Labrador

When I was but thirteen. *(He stops)*

ABSALOM: *(Claps his hands together)* That's it, father. That's it.

SKIPPER PETE: No, son. No. I've forgot the words.

UNCLE JOHN: Forgot the...ye nivir forgot a word ye spoke or sang in yer whole life. Sing, ye old walrus. Sing. *(He bangs his mug on the table.)*

Pete rises slowly. Takes a few paces. Starts to sing the first two lines again. Stops. Absalom, slowly and unsteadily, goes around the table and down to him. He holds his arm, and the pair slowly start to shuffle their feet. Pete starts the song again, growing in power and intensity. Absalom joins in softly on the end of words. John stops banging his mug and becomes absorbed, murmurs encouragement at intervals.

> I sailed out to the Labrador
> When I was but thirteen,
> Me mother wept to see me leave
> And she began to keen.
> I raised you at my tender breast,
> I loved you deep and strong
> And now I fear, my own true dear,
> The sea will drag you down.
> Oh, the sea will drag you down, my son
> Like your father long ago,
> And I'll be left on the wild shore
> To wander to and fro.

As Pete begins the second verse he holds out his hand to John. John slowly moves forward, and the three now form a kind of misshapen circle swaying, stamping their feet, shaking each other's hands and arms up and down. All three raise their voices in triumph for the chorus at the end of the second verse. For a moment they are all one. All free.

Second verse of song

> I didn't go home that year, boys,
> But stayed out on the sea
> And was down in the West Indies
> When a message came to me.
> "Your mother, she was drownded
> While looking out for ye."
> A wild wave is all her grave
> But still I hear her plea.
>
> Oh, the sea will drag you down, me son
> Like your father long ago
> And I'll be left on the wild shore
> To wander to and fro.

At the end, all three break into chin music, and step dance appropriately. At the end of the dance they stand as in a trance. The woman enters silently right. They don't notice her, holding their trance a moment longer.

WOMAN: *(Very quietly)* Young Jimmy Fogarty's lost. *(No response)* He fell off the wharf. *(And again there is no response)*

The woman moves down a little, speaks with a growing intensity.

WOMAN: John! Ye were here. They's saying ye could have saved him.

With a violent movement, Skipper Pete explodes out of the group and swings on her. John staggers and falls on all fours. Absalom sways but stays upright. Pete raises his arm as if to strike her. She doesn't flinch or move.

SKIPPER PETE: They! Who's they?

WOMAN: Aiden. Lew. Old Mr. Fogarty himself. They say.

SKIPPER PETE: And ye just couldn't wait to bring the news, could ye. *(He turns and stomps to the table)* Absalom, the fish should be ready. *(He sits. He spits)* Daughter. Hop the Lard Jesus out of here.
Absalom shakes his head and moves to the stove, lifts the lid, inspects the fish. Starts to serve the fish.

SKIPPER PETE: John! Come and have to bite to eat. Get on yer feet, man.

The woman goes towards Pete a pace or two. John gets to a sitting position.

WOMAN: But ye could have got there. Just a few yards. And ye were told. But you didn't even try.

SKIPPER PETE: *(Roaring)* Mind yer own business, d'you hear. Blood of mine. Jesus, I'll carry the shame o' ye to the grave. Go tell the others what ye want, but I'll tell ye. *(He lowers his voice, passionately believing what he wants to believe)* The sea wanted him. Old Molly. She took him in her good time. She marked him down. Today, tomorrow, next year... it doesn't matter. She touched him the day he was borned.

The woman stares at him as if for the first time seeing the soul of him. And she is both frightened and horrified. He raises his head and locks eyes with her. Challenging, he suddenly roars:

SKIPPER PETE: John! Ye drunken fool. Yer meal's spoiling.
For a few seconds he holds her with his gaze. She struggles to break the hold. Summoning up the one emotion she has inherited from him but rarely used — hate. It flares up and breaks the spell, rushing her to action. She almost runs to John, still sitting dazedly on the floor, only dimly aware of what has been said, of what's going on.

WOMAN: Ye heard that, did ye? *(She shakes John, bends over him, pouring the words into his ear as if they are hot oil to be used for melting the wax that has deafened him for years.)* So. It's God's will is it, to leave a poor mite like that struggling in the water while two grown men — if I durst call you that — let him drown. All it needed was

77

a walk and a rope. Look at ye. *(She stands up — raging)* He curses the day I was born. But I curse the day I took ye for a man in my bed. Thank God I dropped me son before me time. Did ye ever tell him that. Did ye? Stupid, selfish, drunken....

John has struggled to his feet. One phrase scratches through the fog of his brain....

UNCLE JOHN: Drown? Let him drown? We never let nobody drown — dogfish got'n. Skipper. *(He looks uncertainly round for Pete. Confused. Looks back at his wife)* I never let nobody.... Let who drown?

WOMAN: *(Fiercely)* Jimmy Fogarty, that's who. *(Lets it sink in)* Little Jimmy with the freckles and the foxy hair and the big smile with no front teeth. Well — the waters filled that gap now and the connors'll be mouthing at his eyes. And the pair of ye....

SKIPPER PETE: *(Very sharply)* Absalom!

Throughout this interchange Absalom has been sitting at the table, knife and fork raised, ready to eat the fish but he won't eat until his father does. Slowly he puts the knife and fork down.

ABSALOM: Yes, father?

SKIPPER PETE: Go bale the punt, my son.

ABSALOM: *(Surprised)* But the fish, father.

SKIPPER PETE: *(Surprisingly gentle)* We'll have it when ye get back. Put it in the pot now, back on the stove.

ABSALOM: *(Puzzled, but obedient. Almost to himself)* This morning all shining. When I had that dream of fishes. *(He just pours the fish back and replaces the pot on stove. Turns to Skipper Pete)* Father. It's all broken... the fish.... And this morning it was whole.

SKIPPER PETE: *(Impatient)* It'll keep. Fer Chrissake, it's kept for a year. We'll have it when ye get back. All of us. We'll have it together. When she's gone.

Absalom turns and goes out up stage centre. The woman crosses up to Pete and confronts him across the table.

WOMAN: Ye knew, didn't ye? All the time. The little feller was in beggin' and pleadin' wit' ye. But ye'd filled that fool of mine with your dirty ravings of a dead past. Dead... dead... that past. And now ye've added another little body to yer tally. If we ever find him, we should hang him round your neck, so we should, until he's rotted away like an ould fish.

John crosses up to Skipper Pete, still a bit dazed.

UNCLE JOHN: What are ye saying, woman?

He is confused now. And a little afraid. That recollection which nearly emerged as he looked out at the crowd at the wharf is stirring.

UNCLE JOHN: Say it's not true, Skipper. *(He pauses, struggling)* Tell her. *(He puts an arm round him, as if trying to recapture the truth of the dance)* Tell her! Nobody came. We didn't see nobody. *Pete stands up suddenly, shaking himself free, and goes upstage left, turning his back, looking out of the window.*

WOMAN: *(Softly)* He can't tell you. He only lies in the head. But never out loud. Never. *(Shouts)* Go on! Tell him! Tell him that nobody came! That Jimmy Fogarty didn't drown! That ye didn't know! *Skipper Pete does not move.*

UNCLE JOHN: *(An agonized shout)* Skipper! *A silence. In the silence the fog drifts away and John confronts the truth he always knew....*

UNCLE JOHN: My God. *(A pause)* He did come.*(A pause)* The little feller. *(A pause)* Pulling at me leg. *(A pause)* Shouting, he was. *(Horrified at himself)* Why didn't I go. Why didn't we.... *(He crosses up behind Skipper Pete)* Skipper. Why didn't we — hear him. Why? *(No response from Skipper Pete. Suddenly, like a man demented, John spins him round.)* Ye've got to say, Skipper. This is real. We owe it to him. Young Fogarty. We owe it to us. You owe me! *(Pete stares at John, crosses down below him to the table. Pours himself a drink.)*

SKIPPER PETE: I don't owe ye a thing. *(Spins on him)* Don't ye ever fergit it. I don't owe a living soul a thing.

WOMAN: No. They're all dead, that's why. Your bad debts are people, and they're all dead.

Absalom enters from the rear. In his arms he carries Jimmy Fogarty. He is quite happy and excited.

ABSALOM: Look, father. Look what I caught by the side of the boat.

WOMAN: Oh, Lord bless us.

ABSALOM: I nivir caught a boy before. *(He advances down stage towards his father)* What shall I do wid'n, Father. *For a moment all are paralysed, a terrible tableau. Then the woman rushes out calling ...*

WOMAN: *(Off)* Aiden....Aiden....Lew....They've found him. Absalom's found him... they've found him....

Absalom is facing Skipper Pete, the dead boy in his arms. The grandson he might have had! Skipper Pete puts out his hand slowly, traces the blind, wet face with his horny hands. Then he turns, the hand that touched the dead child's face to his throat, as if it is a weight that will choke him. He crosses John and goes back up to the window, facing out. Two men, Aiden and Lew, come in right. They are both wearing waders which are wet. They pause a moment.

AIDEN: *(Advancing slightly)* Here, Absalom. Here, boy. *(A silence. Absalom looks uncertainly between the men and the turned back of his father.)*

AIDEN: Bring him to me, Absalom.

There is an element of urgent anger in his voice. Outside, the murmur of a crowd, men and women. John crosses quickly, and restrains Aiden who is about to move to Absalom to take the boy from him.

ABSALOM: What shall I do, father?

A silence.

LEW: *(In a whisper — as if anything louder would snap a thread that seems to have tied them all and provoke violent reaction)* Fer Chrissake, John. We've got to do something.

ABSALOM: He is mine, isn't he, father. I caught him. I nivir caught a boy before. Can I have him?

A silence. Is there a quiver from Pete? John crosses slowly to Absalom.

UNCLE JOHN: Go wid them, Absalom. Ye can take him. Ye caught him. Go on now. *(Gently he turns him in the direction of the door)*

ABSALOM: Father.

UNCLE JOHN: Don't matter what he says. Not any more. Anyways, he don't know nothing about boys. Only fish. Go on now. *(Slowly he propels Absalom towards the door. He crosses the two men and goes on out. Lew follows him. Aiden turns to go, then turns back.*

AIDEN: We want to talk to ye John. And Skipper, there.

UNCLE JOHN: Aye. I know.

Aiden goes out. John turns.

UNCLE JOHN: Skipper, are ye coming? *(No answer)* Skipper? No — they's nothing out there, b'y. *(No answer)* I 'low it wasn't too bad a day after all, Skipper. One hell of a catch. But I don't think I'll be shareman wid ye any longer. *(He is nearly crying)* I'm going home, ye see. Home.

He pauses — one last time waiting for a response, or any indication from Pete that they have ever known each other at all. But there is nothing. John crosses to the killick. Picks it up. Goes to the door right. And then, a flash of the old sardonic mirth returns.

UNCLE JOHN: I'm taking the killick. I'm going to tie it to me goddamn leg, that's what. In Memoriam, dat's what they say....

He goes out. The murmur of the crowd dies away. After a pause Pete turns. Slowly goes across right and shuts the door. He pauses. Comes across to stove, checks it for flame. Checks the fish. Goes back up stage and disappears partially from view as he undoes and fastens the upstage door. There's just a shaft of light left now coming in through the church window. He goes right and finds an oil lamp, lights it and puts it on the table. He begins to sing... two or three lines of the opening song. Stops. Takes the fish off the stove, fills his plate and begins to eat....

THE END.

Props

The following list of props may be of help for productions far removed from the fishing culture of Newfoundland.

Splitting table
Trap barrels
Pot-bellied stove
Killick
Knitting needles
Splitting knife
Heading knife
Oil stone
Drawing bucket
One kettle for tea
One large saucepan for cooking fish
Four mugs
Four wine bottles, corked with twisted paper for moonshine
Several hanks of rope
Can (an illegal still)
Twine for knitting net, binding killick
Kindling, birch junks
Assortment of floats, gaffs, nets, lobster pots, fish boxes, etc. for set
    dressing
Codfish, six per performance, weighing 10 or more pounds each.
    Should be "round, head on".

The first public performance of the play took place in the Arts and Culture Centre, St. John's, Newfoundland on Wednesday, March 4th, 1973, with the following cast:

Skipper Pete ....Clyde Rose

Uncle John ....Pat Byrne

Rachel (the Woman) ....Flo Edwards

Absalom..Dick Buehler

Children ....Kelly Buehler

Paul Kelly

Perry Fowler

Lew ....Geoff Seymour

Aiden...Leslie Mulholland

****

Set Design ....John Roddis

Lighting ....Tony Duarte

Sound ....Sharon Buehler

Stage Manager ....Pat Wright

Director ....Tony Chadwick

Theresa's Creed

A monologue.

Dedicated to Mary Frances Decker because the play is her, I guess.
       Michael Cook.

The lights rise on Therese's kitchen. There are no containing flats, shape and structure are suggested by pieces of two by four. The artifacts, not the surroundings, must dominate our attention. A tub washer sits downstage left: behind it, centre, a sink — the black plastic pipe drains the water beneath the house. A kitchen chrome set, table and chairs, occupies the area right. It is littered with debris from a family breakfast. From one of the pieces of two by four there hangs a wall phone. The others may contain outlets for appliances. Extreme left, there may be the suggestion of a porch which leads to the entrance. In the porch are four or five ten gallon plastic buckets filled with water. Extreme right, a shelf, big enough to contain an electric kettle and a canister and a mug or two is attached to one of the exposed ribs of the kitchen. Therese is a largish woman in her mid forties. Although the strain of raising a large family on a fisherman's income shows on her face and the occasional weariness that overcomes her, she has much energy and fire, and her eyes still project the image of a young girl on occasions. As the play opens she is shouting from the doorway at her children.

THERESE: Marvin.... Marvin. Ye hear me, now. Stop in to Miss Millie's on yer way back from school and keep her company fer a bit.*(A pause.)* I don't give a shit what ye wants to do, boy, do as yer told. Bernice. *(Shrilling)* Bernice. Stop to Cull's, will ye, an' bring me a pound o' bloney. And don't ye go charging no more cookies to me account. I'm wise to ye, girl. Yis, and tell her I'll be in to settle on Sat'day.

There is the sound of a school bus drawing up...distant shouts, the bus drawing away. Therese comes in from the porch area... pushing her hair out of her eyes....

THERESE: Oh my. Some days.... Well, I'd best git on. *Crosses to the washer, takes out the lead, together with a box of washing powder and a plastic bleach bottle. She plugs the lead into an outlet, crosses to the porch, brings in a ten gallon pail of water and, with an effort, lifts it and empties it into the tub. Takes the bucket back to the porch. Half fills it from another, returns and empties that in, too. She pours soap powder into the washer.*

THERESE: Dats a blessed relief now, washing in cold water. Times I'd spend half the day trying to heat enough to do one washer load.

She adds bleach, crosses to the outlet.

THERESE: 'Tis already plugged in. I swear I'll fergit me head next.

She turns the washer on. Its strange, regular thumping sound is reminiscent of a heartbeat... she puts the lid on to stop the water splashing out... goes downstage and looks out.

THERESE: And it'll rain now, I suppose, and me with neither clothes clean fer the youngsters and it graduation in a few days.... *She disappears upstage into darkness, emerges almost immediately with a hugh armload of clothes. she dumps them down and begins to sort them out... whites in one pile, coloured another.*

THERESE: Though why I should bother about 'em graduating, the Lord only knows. Sometimes I thinks 'tis only foolishness. If their father were alive now, it might be different.

She loads the washer with whites, puts the lid on.

THERESE: And 'tis not as if they even care what they does wi' their life. Time was when they was no choices. We nivir had no choice. If ye was a boy ye got thrown into manhood afore ye was wet behind the ears, no matter how hard the mothers prayed for 'em to be something other than fisherman, walking the water every day. And we. *(Laughs)* I minds me mother to this day. I wor coming up fifteen an' it wor as close as she ever come to giving me a lesson on the facts o' life. Weren't necessary I suppose. We all knew what we had to be the time we was nine or ten. Aye. I wor gitting ready to leave school dat year. Grade 8 I wor in. Stopped me one morning as I wor about to step through the door. Looks at me long and hard an' nods, satisfied. "Ye're alright, maid" she said. "Ye'll do. Ye're good looking enough to git a good man, not like some wi' squish mout's and eyes that had to settle fer a man old enough to be their fathers, aye, and ye're not dat beautiful as ye'd catch all and mebbe none be the end o' it." *(Laughs again.)* No. We 'ad no choice, none at all. Mebbe 'tis a good thing. Though I'm sure I don't know anymore whats good and what isn't fer anybody.

She crosses to the table, sits, pours herself a cup of tea, and lights a cigarette. She's not really used to them. It's a habit she's picked up recently. Out of a sense of bravado or simply defiance, a wish to do something which has met with disapproval from her family all her life. She puffs as a teenager puffs....

THERESE: I suppose we never had time to think, neither. Work afore school, work after in the house, then helping wi' the fish or about the gardens. Git out once in a while fer a walk on Sat'day, get to a dance, mebbe. Meet some young feller ye've known all yer life but somehow 'tis different, and him wit' eels in his feet an' the Divils grin and there ye is... staring up at the stars one night and him doing whatever he wants and knowing 'tis all writ up dere in dem stars from dat time on. The journey to the alter an' the swelling stomach an' the round o' cooking and washing and making fish and cutting wood an' berry picking in the fall. And den the work gits in the way o' the play till it seems there never was none, no, an it be useless to grieve fer, as the priest says, we'se only born to work and sorrow in dis life. I mustn't mind, though, 'tis not all been torment, and I had it better than me mother an' dey, dats a fact. I minds her telling me once about me being borned. She wor helping me Grandfather on the stage, me father wor gone to the Labrador dat year. All I minds of him now is the smell o' tobaccy and the hard voice when he spoke, and dat weren't often. She begun to feel the pains right strong, and her water broke, right dere on the stage head.

"I got to go, Father," she tells 'n.

"Christ, maid," he says, "what fer".

"To born the baby," she says.

He grunts den, and after a bit says, "If ye must ye must, I suppose, but don't ye be too long". An' she pushed herself up the path to the house, and Mary Ellen come den as had borned most of us and me mother had the hot water and the towels laid out be the time she got up and I wor just about t'rough. Dat wor morning. Be the time the day had done wor' out she wor back again wi' him on the stage. Feared to deat' o' him she were. But my, she had beautiful hair. Black it wor. Right down to her arse. I minds playing wi' it as a girl, combing it for her. She sitting and rocking be the old stove, half crooning to herself, and me brushing, brushing 'til her head gleamed, and it didn't seem to belong in dat crowded little house. Woodsmoke an' the smell o' dried fish and me grandfather's tobaccy... Target, it wor... dat belonged. But not me mother's hair. It wor like something in books. Something in dreams a long time ago. I minds right up to the time she wor dying... it wor streaked wi' grey den, but still long and thick... she'd wish fer me to do her hair. "D'ye minds when it wor all black, girl"... she'd say, "All shining... and ye'd sit an' do me hair on a summer's evening"? *(She pauses.)* It wor like another part o' her dat never belonged to the dried fish, the wood smoke, the labour at the stage head. Mine wor nivir like dat. More like me father's, I s'pose. Stringy, tough. Pat used to tell me 'twere like a witches broom. *(She laughs. Pats her hair.)* She told me her hair come from her mother. She wor supposed to have had the most beautiful hair in the whole of Ireland but it fell out on the ship coming over... some disease or other, I don't mind which it wor now. Till the day she died she wore a bandana. Even when they laid her out she had on a bandana. Red, wi' white spots on it. Foolish, the way some t'ings sticks in yer head. Oh, my. Dis won't git me nowhere, I suppose. *She gets up and crosses to the washer, turns it off. Crosses to the porch, comes back with a large plastic bowl used as a washing basket. She puts it down and begins to take garments from the washer and put them through the wringer.*

THERESE: I suppose I'll keep going now 'til dey's all gone. 'Tis a strange business. Ye spends yer life raising a fambly, an' just when dey seems ready to be friends dey's off and running like the Devil was at their tail. Dats how it was wi' the others, anyway, and I doubt dem dats left'll be much different. And when dey's gone, where are ye? Alone in a house full o' empty bedrooms and chipped dishes and a few pictures stuck on the cabinet to remind ye of where yer life went. If Pat wor alive, now, I suppose t'ings'd be a mite different. I don't know though. Seems like he knew all along it wor hardly worth it. "It'd be nice maid", he said... *(Pauses... struggling for the recollections...)* "It'd be nice"... *(Pauses)* Dats right. Come on to snow in the evening... first snow o' winter, and it blowing strong from the nor east enough to freeze the marrow of ye. I allus hates to see that first snow...'tis like the winter settling down on yer like an ould coffin lid and ye still alive, banging away inside...*(She pauses... the wringer grinds on...)* 'Tis such a short time afore the snows come. *(The wringer grinds on... she breaks from her memories with a start.)*

THERESE: Oh my, dere I goes again....
She delves into the tub for more clothes to put through the wringer comes up with Bernice's bra and panties. Holds them up.... Pauses.

THERESE: And I don't suppose she'll be long now afore she's at it... if she isn't already. Blessed Virgin, 'tis a worry. She but fifteen and dey thinks I don't know how they feels or what dey does only now 'tis the backs o' cars and not down be the stage head or up on the hills o' nights. And wi' Pat gone and her big brothers I doesn't seem able to hold her. Seems like wi' no men at home dey goes crazy. We allus held off till the last minute, till we was sure of 'em. And ye can be sure we was den, fer if ye got into trouble, an' most of us did, it seems, then it wor between famblies... got nothing to do with ye or he at all and whether ye wanted to or no it was up to the alter wi' ye, girl. Ye've made yer bed and now ye must lie on it. Aye, and even afore dat, if ye confessed it, and ye knows ye had no choice about dat either, den the priest would ask when ye was coming to see'n about the banns, and dat after giving ye enough penance to keep ye on yer knees for a week. We t'ought we was free, but, ach, we was no better off then an ould

cod... everywhere ye runs dey's a trap somewhere. And we too foolish
to mind'n or look where we was going at all. I doesn't know about
Bernice though.

She puts her clothes through the wringer, fishes for more.

THERESE: Times change and dey ain't nothing anyone can do
about dat. But I knows dey got no thought o' marriage or be spoken fer
it anyways. I got her life threatened. "Don't ye come home to me
Missy," I tells her, "pregnant, because I'm not raisin' no more
youngsters." "I knows what I'm doing", she says, saucy as a black.
"Yis, maid", I tells her, "an' I, too, knows what yer doing wi' that Sam
Pollock, and him a Protestant". In my day ye had to confess dat too, if
ye talked to a Protestant, dat's if ye were alive to tell the tale after yer
father or yer brothers found out. "Why, mam", she says laughing to me
face, "yer some old fashioned. Nobody cares fer dem things anymore,
only old Father Sullivan and he's too foolish to talk about". "Ye minds
yer mout'", I tells her, "talking of a priest dat way". Ah, but dey got no
respect fer nothing dese days. An' I suppose dey don't care who's who
or what's what and dats a good thing in some ways fer as I minds it, it
wor always causing trouble one way or another. But the way dey
carries on, her and dem like her, dats whats foolish, fer they've all
their lives running ahead o' 'em and all it takes is to open yer legs once
too often fer a feller who doesn't give a good goddamn fer anything, let
alone ye, and dey's half of it gone, an' the shame of it on ye, and the
pain of it on ye, too soon be half, and yer girlhood gone like a flower cut
wi' the frost.

*She turns off the wringer, fills the washer again, puts the lid on and
switches on. She picks up the pan of clean clothes and moves to the
doorway.*

THERESE: Well, drat dat. 'Tis raining cats and dogs and me wi' a
full washer load yit. I knows I should a' done it yesterday, but oh my,
me back wor some bad.

*She crosses the kitchen to extreme right, and unhooks a pulley rope
from one of the pieces of two by four. A clothes rack is lowered. She
fastens the rope and begins to load the clothes on to the rack.*

THERESE: I should git down to the Doctor wid'n I suppose, but
they're some stunned. All dey wants to do is poke around in yer
privates, scrape dis, scrape dat, and what the Lord dats got to do wi'
me back I don't know, unless it comes from spending too much time on
it as a maid... *(Laughs).* I'm some shocking... Mary Francis now, me
eldest daughter, she's always on about it. "Ye needs a hysterectomy",
she says, whatever dat is. Ever since she married dat teacher feller

from the mainland she's got right bossy. "Yer draining away", she says, "dey'll be nothing left o' ye be the time yer fifty". "So what", I says, "ye'll all be gone den and what should I care". *(She arranges more clothes.)* Though if Bernice gits herself into trouble I suppose I'll be kept busy fer a bit... they'll be something to keep me... Oh, but dats a terrible way to think. I suppose they means well. And worried, I allow, about being left to care fer me, but I tells dem I'll take care o' meself until me time comes, like Miss Millie. *(She hauls up the pulley, and once again goes to the table and lights up a cigarette).* And den, when Jack, me eldest, wor home last on leave from the Forces all o'em was at me to git married agin. *(Laughs).* "Yer still good looking, mam," they says. *(Laughs self consciously, smoothes down her hair).* Yis, I suppose I am, hair like a witches broom having borned ten youngsters wi' eight living, thanks be to God. An' what would I be doing wi' another man? They was ever only one man fer me, and it might sound foolish to dem dese days. Sure they has more men be the time dey's twenty than Patsy O'Hare and dey says she took on the whole fishing fleet one season... dat was afore Father McCarthy got a holt to her and she seen the light and went to become a nun. *(Pause).* It do git a bit lonely in bed at night times, when ye just wants to talk or turn in to the feel o' a man, the smell o' him. The hardness o' him, legs like an old spruce, hard and bent from a lifetime balancing on boats. I has Bernice in now fer company, but 'tis not the same. Times when I 'as to turn from her, when I feels like crying.

She pauses, a tear gathers in the corner of her eye. She wipes it with her sleeve.

THERESE: Ach. Give over dat old foolishness, maid, the days is full o' work yit, and ye didn't have it as hard as yer mother and dey, suppose yer man has upp'd and gone. He wor good to ye while he wor alive, according to his lights, and dats more den some kin say.... But I'll not be marrying agin. Dats all gone now.... Dat part o' me is all gone now and if I does hunger sometimes... 'tis soon passed *(The phone rings, startling, loud, she puts out her cigarette and crosses to it).* Hello.... Yis, maid, I'm doing a bit o' wash but the Lord knows when I'll git it dry.... It do. Well I might get it out by an' by, den. *(A pause).* Yes, I did see it. *(Pause)* Well, I'd kill dat. I've never seen the like fer cheating on a maid. *(A pause).* No, girl, I don't think she will. But if 'twas me I'd leave'n an' dats a fact. *(A pause).* I knows, maid, some crooked, dat one, wi' all her money. What good does it do 'em? If I wor to turn like dat when I got old I'd give up. *(A pause).* Oh, she's canny though. She's trying to git her hooks into dat lawyer, I kin see that, he'd better watch hisself. *(Pause)* True enough, girl.... butter wouldn't melt in her mout', but he must be some stunned if he can't see t'rough the sherry and cookies she serves him. *(A pause)*. I don't know who killed'n, maid, I'm sure. But I knows the young feller didn't do it. Ye kin tell be his face. My, he's some good looking. *(A pause. She laughs)*. I dare say I wouldn't push him out o' bed, maid. *(Pause)*. Push him to the wall?... *(Laughs)* ye're some shocking. Well, alright den. *(A pause)*. I might.... Ye kin give me a call later... oh... Lill, how's yer mother. *(A pause)*. She is. *(Pause)*. I heard tell of a feller down the motel was selling silver medals fer dat. *(Pause)*. Ye wears it all the time, maid, and its supposed to be just wonderful fer the arthritis.... Well, ye knows how crippled Big Mick wor, his hands jest like pig's knuckles. Well, he's been wearing one dis week, and Mary says she's nivir seen him looking so spry dis year. He wor out chopping wood fer her yestiday. *(Pause)*. Dats true enough, too.... I told her yestiday she'd have to watch'n. Next thing the noisy old welfare officer'll be round telling'm to git to work, ye knows how dey is. Yis, well, alright, maid. I'll talk to ye later.

She hangs up the phone, crosses to the washer, turns if off, starts the wringer and begins to put the clothes through.

THÉRÈSE: I jest loves that *Edge o' Night*. Only bit o' time I 'as to meself all day, jest afore the youngsters come home. I used to watch dat fambly court all the time too, but sure 'tis not like a court at all. I nivir seen a judge like dat one... puffing away at dat stinking old pipe, and acting like God the Father almighty on a good day when everyone knows He 'as bad days like the rest o' us. I minds when I 'ad to go up dat time wi' Walter, when he wor caught bringing dat caribou home. Pat wor some proud o' him, and him but thirteen. "Don't ye mind dem, boy", he says. "Bunch o' idiots, dats what dey is. What do dey want to bring dem beasts to the island fer if its not to gi' folks a chanct o' a meal o' meat now and agin. Aye, and meat dey can't afford to buy, fer the price dey pays fer fish be not enough to keep a scarecrow alive. Dey can rob a poor man blind", he says, "but God helps dose what tries to help theyselves and keep 'em off'n the Welfare. S'pose they means to keep 'em fer damn tourists," he said. *(She pauses)*. Funny really.... Pat wor like dat. Speak to the Divil in his own house, not afeard o' man nor beast, but the minute he got t'rough the door it wor like he wor a different man. Do anything to avoid trouble. It'd be "Yes, sir, good morning, sir", an' dey doing terrible tings to'n, cheating him on his fish and charging too much fer his gear, yit on the water he wor like a lion. I've nivir seen him afeard... no, and dey was times I was wid'n, when I wor younger, helping him haul the traps I t'ought the sea would swallow us up fer sure an' him whistling away, not giving a damn. He wor never happier den when he wor on the water. Seemed like the boat wor a part o' him, and he and the boat wor a part o' the water. I suppose he wor free den. That was it. He never knowed dat dat wor when I loved'n most. And dats the time I suppose, when he niver cared what or who I wor as long as I kept me place and did as I wor told. *(A pause).* But just let'n walk out o' the house....*(She wrings a few more clothes.... pauses again....)* He nivir went to the court wi' Walter. I 'ad to go. And the old feller on the bench — well I nivir seen such a miserable looking creature in all me life... he looked like a sculpin 'ad bin pickled in brine fer a week. And pickled... I suppose dats what he wor... ye could smell him all over the court house. An' when our time come he called me up, not Walter. "Yer son was caught flagarente delicto", he says "does ye know what dat means"? Now where in the name of all dat's Holy had I bin all me life to know what dat meant. "No, sir," I says, saucy I wor. "And I doesn't think I wants to know." He gets nasty den. "Yer son is a minor, Mrs. Moriarty," he says, "and therefore ye're responsible fer his crime."

"And what crime is dat, your Honor"? I asks. "We've a house full o' mout's to feed and little enough to manage on, an' he acted like a man to git some meat fer us."

Dere was some tittering in court den, I tells ye, and he banged with the hammer something fierce, den made a face as if it hurt'n... I 'low he had a hangover, fer he wor to the merchant's the night afore and ye may be sure they weren't short of a drop dere... planning what to do wi' us all I expect... Walter and his caribou, and dem as 'adn't paid dere bills and the few what got into fights.

"'Tis stealing, mam"(he says to me.) "Dat caribou is the property of the Crown, and in any case yer son 'ad no licence."

"We can't afford no licence, Sir," I says then, "and I doubts if the Queen'd come all the way from Buckingham Palace or wherever it is she's to, to check on one skinny caribou.... Sure", I says, "Dey's hardly enough grass here to feed dat, 'tis a mortal sin to let'n roam. Uncle Jack Penton now, he found the bones o' t'ree on'm on the upper side of the arm, starved to death dey was." Well, the court was going some, I tell ye, and some were cheering and shouting out and he got redder'n a turkey in the face. "No doubt he did," he shouts. "No doubt. And I don't doubt but the meat was on dem bones 'ad already found its way into the Moriarty stomachs, and dem like ye, for dere's no caribou living," he says, "couldn't live in dem barrens with all the moss and lichen dat's up there. Fined twenty five dollars," he says "and bound over to keep the peace in your charge, mam." *(She laughs)* Twenty five dollars! I asked'n den, meek and mild if I could pay it off be the week. He softened at dat and asked what I 'ad in mind. "Ten cents, Sir," I said. And he banging away wi' that old hammer again and wincing, and shouting fer the Mountie to clear the court. Well, the upshot o' it was dat all o' Walter's fishin' money went to pay'n off dat year. And Pat, when he heard what I done, he laughed. Den he swore on me fer shaming'n. Den he laughed agin. Funny though, how he wouldn't go. The sea and the creatures in it... dat wor the only world fer him. The rest o' it wor a millstone.... Aye, and me, too at times. He told me once he hated me. That wor later mind, when they didn't seem much laughter left in 'n. I took dat some hard, I tells ye. But it woren't me he hated. I knows dat.... It wor being alive wi' all them people living off'n, putting ye down, scorning ye fer what ye was. An' the fish gone, or most of it anyways, and me worrying about money from one day to the next. Dey was so many of 'em to look out to. An' it seemed like I was always reminding him of how he failed us somehow, dough God knows I understood, I didn't mean dat. I wonders now, if he understands we at all. *(She loads the second wash into the basket).* Lill says the sun'll be out by an' by. P'raps I'll jest leave 'em till it clears up. *(There are a few clothes left. She puts them in the tub).* An' dat waters black now, but it'll have to do fer what's left. *(She starts the washer again, replaces the lid).* At least I got no woollens to worry about today. Dat nylon's a wonderful t'ing. Washes out like new every time. Dey was a time when I 'ad to do the half o' it be hand. My, and dem heavy sweaters Pat used to wear, stiff wi' all dat old gurry....

Picks up the pan of washing and takes it to the porch, puts it down comes back. Gets a floor cloth from under the sink... wipes around the base of the washer.

The wash don't take no time now, thanks be to God. When I 'ad 'em at home now, eight youngsters and Pat 'an me Mother, God rest their souls, it'd be twice a week, all day, and five lines weighted wi' wash. Dats some sight on a fine day. The clothes dancing, and a smell off 'em like the wind scented. Coming across all dem old woods I suppose... picking up the wild blossoms. *(She replaces the floor cloth).* All dat silly old stuff dey tells ye on television to put into yer wash now, and to make it smell fresh. Sure, dey's nothing like a summer wind. What could be sweeter dan dat. Though I suppose they doesn't get summer winds, dem dat lives in cities. *(She crosses right, plugs in the electric kettle, stands by it waiting).* I wor to Toronto, onct. Dat wor when

Walter wor stationed at Trenton. My, dey got some lovely shops dere. I could spend all day just walking about dem, looking. *(Laughs).* Though where people gits the money from to buy dat stuff I doesn't know. Be the time I pays fer the grocery each week, an' puts a bit by to git their clothes fer the winter dey's hardly enough fer the oil. And here I am, needing a new blower fer the stove, and God knows we'll freeze the winter if we don't get'n and the Welfare says 'tis not their job an' they pays me enough to look after t'ings like that. And where be the Blessed Virgin am I to git seventy dollars wi' no man working, and two hundred and eighty a month wi' four growing youngsters to school, and the price o' t'ings as dey is.

The kettle has boiled. She takes a mug, puts a teabag into it, and carries the tea across to the table where she sits. Lights a cigarette.
'Tis a question of who ye knows, dats all. Madeline Peak now, up the road, she got her house done top to bottom, new clapboard and new roof and brand new wood and oil stove, and her sons sending her money from the States, and God knows how much she got salted away, fer ye knows dat old man Peak had money when he died... Christ. He nivir paid his sharemen but one half of their wages and dat when he wor bringing home t'ousands o' fish. Dey says she got it in a box under the floorboards in her bedroom. Aye, and the way t'ings is now, it won't be long afore some fellers wi' a few in'll surprise her some night, her and her box. Olga now, she says dat the Welfare Officer spent days, aye nights too, down there wi' her afore she got the work done, and she should know, living at the back of'n. And I allows he did, too, fer no other woman on the island would look at'n, wi' his watery pigs eyes, an' a nose on him worse than Cracky Hines, poor feller, and him dead these ten years and nivir knowing a maid on account o' it. *(Laughs).* I minds Pat now, and Jack and dey, one night afore Christmas, and dey well on wi' the shine, tormenting Cracky something terrible about it. "Dey says a big nose means a big cock", says Pat, sly, winking at the others. Oh, he could be the Divil when he wanted... *(she laughs)...* And poor old Cracky, grinning and nodding dat great big nose o' his like a port light winking away. "Dats right". And den Jack started 'em singing, and dey all knows dat Cracky couldn't sing to save his life, no, nor wouldn't neither, fer he was too shy be half. And it wor sing or show yer piece.... *(Laughs again).* Oh my. And Pat gits a ruler an' says, "Out wi' it Cracky... on the table wid'n... what is it now, six." "Eight, at least" says Jack, eyeing Cracky's nose, "Eight or ten, I'd say", and Cracky nodding and grinning, fearful embarrassed. "No," cries Pat... "twelve den, we'll try

twelve, come on, out wid'n," and den Cracky near crying shouts out: "What's de good o' showing it, fer dere's no-one would have I anyways." 'Twas a mortal sin to torment him so. *(Laughs again).* Dey gives up after dat, an' we nivir did git to see'n and Cracky nivir got to use'n I suppose and dats dat. But that Madeline Peak — she'd do anything, now, to git what she wants, and I allows dats just what she did, fer what other reason could they be fer her to git all dat done and me with neither blower, and hardly a stick o' wood cut and the price o' t'ings scandalous.... Dey's times, so they is, when I don't know as how I wants to keep on wi' it. P'raps Pat got the best of it after all. He looked happy enough laid out dere in the living room... smile on his face so much as to say... "I made it, ye see... I got rid of it all now... all the torment and worry of it"... *(She pauses near tears again).* But I'd give anyt'ing to hear him singing "The Gay Spanish Maid", like he always done when he 'ad a few in, and the boys was all gathered and Jack had the accordian going....

Didn't seem to matter den dat we got nothing. We was all together den. An' everyone in the place the same as we, but 'tis as if now we's all separated, like the cream from the milk. Nobody sings no more. Nobody comes to visit since Pat been gone. All the youngsters wants is skiddoos and cars and I can't say as 'ow I blame 'em, fer everyone else got one or t'other or both, though God knows how they pays fer 'em at all. Jack's accordian, now, 'asn't bin used dese five years. 'Tis up there in the attic, gatherin' dust. I goes up sometimes, just to look at'n, to see if its still dere, an' the dust dat t'ick I'm afeared to touch it... 'Tis like all dats left is memories. If I wor to clean it now, and bring it down, 'twould be no use to no-one. It'd be jest an ornament... 'tis better where it be. *(The phone rings, it startles her, she jumps up).* My. Dat wash'll be done to death. *(She hurriedly crosses to washer, turns it off, crosses to phone).* Hello.... Yis, maid.... *(A pause).* No, I'm about finished. 'Tis stopped, 'as it. No... I weren't looking out, maid. *(Pause).* Yis, girl. Last week when I come home there wor Bernice and Marvin and dat crowd from the bottom smooching away in the living room wi' the lights off and dat ole record player roaring away... I'm like to take dat down to the cove afore the summers out. An' the two young ones looking on, maid. *(A pause).* I tells 'em, 'tis not right, such goings on in the house in front o' youngsters, but dey takes no notice o' me, maid, not since Pat's gone. I'm dreading school turning out and dats a fact.... *(A pause).* Well, I swears, if I took a broom handle to Marvin like I used to do wi' his brother when dey was up to mischief he'd crack me over the 'ead wi' it. And Bernice.... Whatever would Pat 'ave made of it, at all. *(A pause).*

I suppose yer right, maid. Dey get at it whatever we says and dey's a chance of 'em drawing the line in the house, I suppose. *(Pause)* Now ye knows I'd love to go. *(Pause)*. Well, I wor just two numbers off the jackjot last week, twelve hundred dollars. My, what couldn't I do wid dat. *(Laughs)* Well, I wor sitting dere, maid, waiting, oh, it must've been fer at least ten numbers, waiting fer a rotten ole nine. The sweat wor pouring off me. I'lows if they called it I'd have fainted right away. *(Laughs)*. Tell him to blow at the top den, about eight. Yis, girl, alright, I'll be ready.

Puts the phone down, crosses to the washer, begins to put the last few things through the wringer.

Dats an awful lot o' money, now, twelve hundred dollars. If I wor to win dat I could tell the old Welfare Man to stuff his blower up his arse. *(Pauses)*. Den I could git in to Gander, mebbe, and buy the youngsters dere new outfits fer the winter.... They're growing some fast, I swears I can't keep up wi' 'em at all, and dey isn't content anymore wi' hand me downs... they wants nothing but the best, and here's me wi' nothing. It'd be nice, dough, if I were to win jest a part o' it. Could git a quarter o' meat and me flour fer the winter an' a deep freeze fer the fish, dat'd be some nice. And if dere was anyt'ing left den, I could git some nice material fer Lillian to make me a new dress. She makes lovely clothes. Her crowd o' girls, now, always looks as if dey just come from the pages o' a catalogue. *(Dreams)*. And den I could put some money by to say Masses fer Pat and me Mother.... P'raps Mary Francis could git a nice sung mass fer 'em in the cathedral in St. John's.... Dat'd be lovely. I minds we used to have 'em as a maid. Dat wor when Father McCarthy wor young and 'ad a choir. He wor an old guilderoy in someways, but he kept a lovely choir dem days. *(She is silent)*. But whats the pint in dreaming, girl? Ye've nivir won anyt'ing in yer life and I allows yer not about to. But I'll go to the Bingo anyways. Tis a bit o' company... 'bout all any o' us gits dese days. Dey says the church takes too much out o' it.... I doesn't know why folks is surprised.... Dey've always taken too much to my mind from dem dat can least afford it. I minds Father McCarthy when all of us girls was taking classes fer confirmation... "'Tis blessed to be poor", he'd tell us. "Ye'll git yer reward in Heaven". Poor old soul. I suppose he wor only trying to help, fer dere's nothing worse den expecting somet'ing ye ain't going to git, and dats a fact.

She had been putting the wrung clothes on the washer lid. Now she takes them and puts them on top of the others. In the porch. She comes

back in carrying an empty bucket and begins to empty the washer.
She sings.

THERESE: The Gay Spanish Maid, at the age of sixteen,
　　　　　Through the meadow she roamed far and wide.
　　　　　Beneath the green tree she sat down fer to rest
　　　　　Wi' her gay gallant youth be her side.

*She stops the pump, carries the bucket to the sink, empties the water
down it, comes back, turns on the pump to refill the bucket, sings on.*
　　　　　My ship sails at midnight, my darling, said he,
　　　　　And with you may I never more roam,
　　　　　Won't ye meet me tonight when yer parents are
　　　　　at rest,
　　　　　Won't ye meet me tonight on the shore?

*She stops the pump, crosses to the sink to empty the bucket... Pauses...
Hums... Pauses.*

I've forgotten most o' dat now. Seems if ye don't keep it up it goes from
ye.

*She frowns, hums... recollects a verse... bends down to get the floor
cloth from beneath the sink and goes back to the washer to wipe the
tub.*
　　　　　The moon, which had risen, shone over the deep,
　　　　　The water and sky seemed to meet
　　　　　But the only sad sound was the murmering waves
　　　　　As they broke on the rock at her feet....

*She has finished wiping the tub, puts the lid on. Pushes it back
towards the sink, dries her hands on a handtowel.*
Ye knows, dats something I've taken to doing meself lately....
Expecting something fer nothing. 'Tis something I've nivir done
before but seems like the whole place be going round wid hands out,
an' 'tis catching. But what can ye do. 'Tis not as if I didn't work, God
knows.... I've nivir known a day when I didn't work and I suppose now
I must sit and wait fer me old age pension as a sign from someone dat
I've done well. And if I lives long enough to git it, I 'lows I'll not live
long enough to enjoy it. Dere's Miss Milly now, hanging on fer grim
deat' 'til she's a hundred so's she kin git a telegram from the Queen.
Yis, an I suppose the Queen lives to be a hundred she'll expect
telegrams from all o' us. Well, she can kiss me arse. 'Tis an awful t'ing
fer a woman on her own when all she do be waiting fer is the
governmint to pay her fer living sixty five years.... I tells Miss Milly
she's foolish, but what kin ye expect when yer middle names
Victoria...?

She unplugs the washer, folds up the cord and puts it inside... crosses to pick up the wash powder and bleach and puts that back inside the washer.

THERESE: But den, dey had it different from us. Dey nivir asked no questions of no one. If dere men died 'twas the will o' God. If dey was no fish, 'twas the will o' God. If dere youngsters was taken sick, and dey was no doctor this fifty mile and much o' that across water, they'd wait for'n to die and dat was the will o' God. Pat... he wor a good Catholic in some ways... drove us all to Mass on Sunday, but I wondered times whether he done it 'cos he always done it, and his father afore him, and give him a link wi' somet'ing. I'm half inclined to to t'ink he didn't believe in the will o' God though. T'ings 'ad 'appened to make him angry. Like de time Joe Green an' his brother went trew the ice an' dey having no business on it at all, fer the wind 'ad come up Westard, and she wor breaking up, and dey wid a few in, but dey was wild, dem two, an' wild fer the taste o' seal meat. It wor Pat went out wi' Jack when it come on dark, to look for'n. I didn't want'n to go fer the sea wor some fierce outside, but he told me to mind me own business. As if he weren't me business, no Jack neither, me first born. "Dey's kin," he said, "And if dey weren't I'd go anyways". An' I sitting wi' the Rosary fer t'ree hours, God help me, fer when its times like dat, ye've nowhere else to run.

First off he told me, dey t'ought dey'd hit a dead head in the water... some t'ree miles out or so, following a lead t'rough the pack. And it breaking up and growlers turning over and it dark and dey taking water so dat Jack wor all the time bailing to keep her up. But it weren't no piece o' timber. It wor Joe. Frozen solid he wor... couple o' feet below the water. They cast about a spell, den, looking for t'other one, but wor like to be lost demselves, so Pat come on back wi' him. Dey nivir did find his brother. Took eighteen hours to thaw'n out so dey could arrange him in his coffin.... And his eyes gone in the time he wor in the water. Pat nivir said a word all night. Sat up an' got drunk, den fell asleep he be the stove an' Jack wor dat wore out he fell asleep on the daybed, oilskins and all. He wor but fifteen den. Den Father McCarthy at the wake says as how we was all brothers o' the sea and must trust God in His Wisdom to hold us, or let us fall when he wanted'n. Pat went redder'n a pot of jam. "God 'adn't not'ing to do wi' it, Father," he says, very quiet. Ye could 'ave 'eard a pin drop, fer dey was all dere. Mary and dey, and the fambly. "It was dem", he said, "and the way it is here, an' who knows but dey didn't want to go dat way, fer there's damn all to keep us". An' dey was just Mary sobbing quiet, no other sound, and Joe in his coffin wi' his eyes bandaged dat folks mightn't be too stricken. He left den. I minds Father McCarthy's face, as white as Pat's wor red. But he said nar' word about it. Not den. Not ever. I wondered, den, if Pat wor half expecting to drown hisself dat night, 'ad jest gone out not caring, though nivir another man in the cove would've launched his boat in dat gale o' wind. 'Tis funny. Ye lives wi' a person all yer life, and ye nivir knows'n. An' if dats true, whats the point of it at all. Is we all to be strangers. 'Tis too cruel to be borned jest fer dat.

She crosses to the table. Lights a cigarette.

THERESE: Funny, how I talks to meself now, and yit all the time Pat wor alive, we nivir talked o' things like dat. We was both too shy I 'llows... dere's youngsters to take yer mind off t'ings, an' the talk o' the days work, men's work mostly, and the worry o' making ends meet, and a bit o' gossip, and when the winter come, the drinking, and the singing, an' the fool tricks we played on each other, like dat time wi' Cracky Hines. I suppose it wor best to leave t'ings be. Oh my. *She gets up and stacks the dishes and takes them across to the sink, dumps them in.*

THERESE: If the weather holds, I must git the boys to turn the garden and put me potatoes in. Though 'tis a torment trying to git 'em to do anyt'ing. If I kin git t'ree sacks the year it'll be a Godsend. I wonders, should I let Morgan go fishing wi' Marvin when schools out. He's awful young but Marvin's a good boy on the water, jest like his brother was. Pat taught 'em well, and dey's no fear in dem at all, though dey's times a bit o' it might stand 'em in good stead. P'raps dey could git enough den to keep theirselves in money the summer, and buy a few clothes maybe. 'Twould be a help. If dey does well, I might take Marvin out o' school next year and den he kin go to night school. Dey pays 'em for doing dat, Lil says. I doesn't know, though. He's doing well at his books and God knows I shouldn't be the one to hold'n back, though 'twould be good to have'n about the house fer a year or two yit to help wi' t'ings. I'm sure I doesn't know what to do wi' Bernice.... She'll nivir make Grade XI the way she carries on. I'm afeared fer her. Time was when ye could git a daughter into service in a nice home, but now dats not good enough fer 'em. Dey wants to be secretaries and hairdressers and I don't know what. Oh well, I suppose she'll git somet'ing by an' by, if she stays out o' trouble. *She pushes the washer back parallel to the sink.*

THERESE: Some expensive, girls. If I 'ad me time back I'd 'ave had all boys. Deys a torment but dey ain't half as much trouble when dey gits to their teens. Still and all, she helps about the house, and I suppose I kin git her to come berry picking wi' me in the Fall. Lill says the price be going up dis year... and so it should. A dollar a gallon I got last year and me out from dawn to dusk on me knees picking, picking until I couldn't see no more, the sun on the berries blinding ye. I swears dat what's wrong wi' me eyes now. Dat old sun on the berries. But 'tis some nice on a good day when ye stops for lunch, the kittle going on a few sticks, and ye looking down over the hill at the water, the men at the handlines den, and the spire o' the old church on Duck Island sticking up whiter'n whalebone. I minds dat time... the year afore Pat died, when dey had Mass out dere. All the families going off in the boats, sun beating the water till it shone like dat old copper pan me mother 'ad, till the feller come from Toronto and give her a couple o' dollars fer it. I minds it well... all the boats stretched out across the ocean fer seven miles, and den anchoring in the cove, and all of us saying hello, and smiling like we were met fer the first time. An' the Church wor full, and we all spilled out on the grass, and the gulls and the murrs and the tansies and the puffins setting up the great din and all around the ocean... nothing but ocean... shining in the sun. Dey says the church be two hundred year old.... I don't know about dat... But the winders are some old fashioned. Dey was right low, ye could see right t'rough the aisle, and from the inside all ye could see about ye was ocean still.... And dere we all was, and the priest 'ad brought loudspeakers wired to some kind o' battery, an' we said Mass out dere, on Duck Island, in the sun, kneeling on the grass. Pat knelt next to me, and Walter and Marvin and Mary Francis... she wor home den, and Morgan and Bernice....

"I believe in God the Father Almighty, Creator o' heaven and Earth and in Jesus Christ his only begotten Son,"

I minds the Creed. An' I looked across at Pat and he wor crying. I nivir durst say anyt'ing to'n. Nivir mentioned it. *(She pauses.)* And after the mass, we all had a picnic, an' the fires was going an' the beer flowing... well, don't say we nivir had a good time. It seemed den it wor the beginning o' something, but I t'inks now, it wor the other way about. It wor the end of it, somehow. We nivir done it agin. And when I gits to the island dese days, once or twice a summer, it makes me sad to t'ink on it. Seemed like we was at the top o' some kind of curve and from den on, it wor all down hill. Pat. He knew. An' I suppose its only jest coming to me. And I'm not sure whether I wants to know about it or not. I should jest git on, I suppose fer a few more years, and not mind nothing, 'til dey've gone. 'Til dey've all left me. I minds how Pat — the week afore he died it wor... I minds how he said — it'd come on to snow something fierce... "It'd be nice, maid", he said, "if, when deys all gone, when all the youngsters on the whole bloody island has upped and gone, if dey was a nice old people's home fer us to crawl into until we dies. Think on it", he said. "Someone fer to wait on ye a bit, git yer meals, wake ye in the morning and tell ye when to git to bed o' nights. Don't ye t'ink dat'd be nice, maid?" An' I said, "I don't know Pat boy, I doesn't know, at all".

THERESE: *(She begins to cry... wipes her tears with her apron).* And dey goes and does it now, dered be no pint in me going on me own, boy, would dere.

She struggles to control herself. Goes down stage looks out.

THERESE: Well, damn dat. 'Tis raining agin. An' I suppose it rains forever dis wash is goin' out. Come on, Therese, girl, come on. Deys no pint in grieving.... none at all. 'Twas long enough ago ye made yer bed, and I 'llows ye've some time left to lie on it....

She crosses to the porch. Picks up the bowl of clothes. Exits.

THE END